HOME LIBRARY

FAVORITE CASSEROLES

& OTHER EXCITING RECIPES

Manufactured in the U.S.A.

ISBN: 0-88176-378-0

Cover Design: Kitty Lam

Contents

Introduction

You, the consumer, made this recipe collection possible by taking certain recipes that first appeared on food product labels or in advertisements and choosing them as your favorites! We have included only quality recipes that are or will soon become family treasures. The recipes are reprinted exactly as they appear on the labels or in the advertisements.

This book contains hundreds of casserole and main dish recipes using meat, poultry, fish, and shellfish plus wonderful egg and scrumptious pasta dishes. We did not want to exclude anyone from the cooking fun, so for the diet watchers we have some recipes that are low calorie, low cholesterol, low sodium and low fat. Microwave recipes are also featured. The recipes range in scope from gourmet-style dishes, such as "Coconut Fried Shrimp," to family favorites, such as "Country Cooking Casserole." We have included American favorites, like "Beef Stroganoff," and international specialties too — "Spaghetti Italiano" and "Teriyaki Shish Kabobs."

To look up your favorite recipe in the index if you do not remember the exact title, look under the brand name or the main food ingredient, such as "chicken."

Any questions or comments regarding the recipes should be directed to the individual manufacturers for prompt attention. All recipes in this book have been copyrighted by the food manufacturers and cannot be reprinted without their permission.

Your meal planning worries are over — open this book to any page and you will have a favorite dish for your family and friends.

Casseroles

Company Chicken Casserole

3 large chicken breasts, split
1 teaspoon salt
¼ teaspoon pepper
2 to 3 tablespoons **PURITAN® Oil**
1 can cream of chicken soup
¾ cup white wine
4-ounce can mushroom stems and pieces, drained
5-ounce can water chestnuts, drained and sliced
2 tablespoons chopped green pepper
¼ teaspoon thyme
Cooked rice, if desired

Preheat oven to 350°. Sprinkle chicken with salt and pepper and brown in hot **PURITAN® Oil**. Place skin side up in an 11½ × 7½ × 1½-inch baking dish. Blend soup into drippings in skillet, then gradually stir in the wine. Add drained mushrooms, water chestnuts, green pepper and thyme. Heat to boiling, then pour around chicken. Cover baking dish with foil. Bake at 350° for 25 minutes; uncover and bake 25 to 35 minutes longer, until chicken is tender. Serve with hot rice, if desired.   *6 servings*

Mexican Chicken Rolls

2 whole chicken breasts, split, skinned and boned
1 4 oz. can whole green chili peppers
4 tsp. chopped olives
½ cup shredded Monterey Jack cheese
1 egg, slightly beaten
1 cup crushed tortilla chips
¼ cup vegetable oil
1 1⅝ oz. envelope enchilada sauce mix
½ cup water
1 16 oz. can **S&W® Ready-Cut Tomatoes**
½ cup shredded Cheddar cheese

Pound chicken breasts to flatten. On each breast, put 1 chili pepper, 1 tsp. chopped olives and 2 Tbsp. Monterey Jack cheese. Roll-up the breasts tightly and secure with toothpicks. Dip each roll into egg, then into crushed chips to coat. Heat oil in skillet and brown chicken rolls lightly. Place rolls in a shallow casserole dish. Prepare enchilada sauce according to package directions, only using ½ cup water and **Ready-Cut Tomatoes**. Pour sauce over chicken rolls. Bake at 350° for 35-40 minutes. Sprinkle Cheddar cheese over top and bake an additional 5 minutes or until cheese is bubbly.   *Serves 4*

Chicken-Cheese Ravioli Casserole

3 tablespoons cooking oil
1 tablespoon butter or margarine
1 broiler-fryer chicken, cut into serving pieces
¼ cup chopped onion
¼ cup chopped green pepper
1 can (6 oz.) sliced mushrooms, drained
2 cans (15 oz. each) **CHEF BOY-AR-DEE® Cheese Ravioli in Beef and Tomato Sauce**
¼ cup chopped pimiento
1 cup light cream
Hot pepper sauce
1 package (10 oz.) Chinese pea pods
3 tablespoons toasted slivered almonds

Combine cooking oil and butter. Heat in medium sized skillet. Fry chicken parts until lightly browned. Remove browned parts to warm platter. Sauté onion and pepper in remaining butter. Add drained sliced mushrooms and **Cheese Ravioli in Beef and Tomato Sauce**. Cover; simmer for 5 minutes. Add pimiento, light cream and hot pepper sauce. Stir gently. Cook Chinese pea pods according to package directions. Add to Ravioli mixture. Arrange chicken on top; cover. Bake for 45 minutes in 350 F oven. Garnish with toasted almonds.   *Serves 4 generously*

Alpine Chicken Casserole

4 cups chopped cooked chicken
2 cups celery slices
2 cups toasted bread cubes
1 cup **KRAFT Real Mayonnaise**
½ cup milk
¼ cup chopped onion
1 teaspoon salt
Dash of pepper
1 8-oz. pkg. **KRAFT Natural Swiss Cheese Slices**, cut
    into cubes
¼ cup slivered almonds, toasted

Combine ingredients except nuts; mix well. Pour into 2-quart
casserole; sprinkle with nuts. Bake at 350°, 40 minutes.

6 servings

To Make Ahead: Prepare the recipe as directed. Cover; refrigerate
several hours. Bake at 350°, 50 minutes. Uncover; continue baking 10 minutes.

Fiesta Casserole

1 can (10¾ oz.) cream of chicken soup
1 jar (8 oz.) pasteurized process cheese spread
2 cups chopped, cooked or canned chicken
1 can (4 oz.) **OLD EL PASO® Chopped Green Chilies**,
    drained
12 **OLD EL PASO® Corn Tortillas**
1 can (10 oz.) **OLD EL PASO® Mild Enchilada Sauce**
1-2 cups shredded lettuce
½ cup chopped tomato

Preheat oven to 350°F. Combine soup and process cheese spread,
mixing until well blended. Add chicken and green chilies. Spread
½ cup of chicken mixture over bottom of a 2-quart rectangular
baking dish. Layer four of the tortillas, dipping each in enchilada
sauce, and one third of the remaining chicken mixture; repeat

layers two more times. Cover with foil; bake 20 minutes. Remove foil, continue baking 15 minutes. Top with lettuce and tomato.

Makes 6 servings

MICROWAVE METHOD:
Microcook uncovered on 70% power for 24 to 27 minutes or until heated through. Turn twice during cooking time.

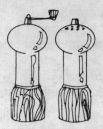

Oriental Chicken and Rice Casserole

1 bag **SUCCESS® Rice**
2 cups cubed, cooked chicken
1 tablespoon soy sauce
2 tablespoons lemon juice
1 can (1-lb.) bean sprouts, drained
1 cup finely chopped celery
¾-1 cup mayonnaise
1 can (5 oz.) water chestnuts, drained and sliced
¼ cup finely chopped green onion
½ teaspoon salt
⅛ teaspoon black pepper
1 can (3-oz.) chow mein noodles

Cook bag of rice according to package directions. Drain. While rice is cooking, sprinkle chicken with soy sauce and lemon juice. Add the bean sprouts, celery, mayonnaise, water chestnuts, onion, salt and pepper. Add the rice. Mix well and pour into a buttered 2-quart casserole dish. Bake, uncovered, at 375°F. for 15 minutes. Sprinkle with noodles. Bake 5 more minutes.

Makes 8 servings (about 1 cup each)

Uncle Ben's® Chicken Casserole With Wild Rice

1 package (6 ounces) **UNCLE BEN'S® Original Long Grain & Wild Rice**
2 cups hot water
1 frying chicken, cut up
Salt and pepper, to taste
1 can (10¾ ounces) condensed cream of mushroom soup
½ cup milk
½ cup slivered almonds
1 tablespoon butter or margarine

Combine contents of rice and seasoning packets and water in a 2½ quart casserole. Season chicken with salt and pepper to taste. Arrange on top of rice mixture. Bake, covered, 1¼ hours at 375 F., or until chicken is tender. Combine soup and milk. Sauté almonds in butter or margarine until lightly browned. Pour soup mixture over chicken in casserole. Sprinkle top with almonds. Return to oven and bake uncovered until hot and bubbly.

Makes 6 servings

Deep Dish Lamb & Biscuits

2 lbs. boneless lamb shoulder, cubed
2 tablespoons salad oil
1 cup chopped onion
1 clove garlic, crushed
2 cups chicken broth
1 teaspoon caraway seeds
½ teaspoon salt
⅛ teaspoon pepper
1 cup sliced celery
1 pkg. (10 oz.) frozen peas and carrots, defrosted
2 tablespoons cornstarch
1 tablespoon cold water
1 cup (8 oz.) **BREYERS® Plain Yogurt**
1 cup biscuit mix
1 tablespoon chopped parsley
⅓ cup **BREYERS® Plain Yogurt**

Brown lamb in oil; add onion and garlic, sauté 5 minutes. Add broth, caraway seeds, salt and pepper. Cover and simmer 45 minutes. Add celery; simmer 15 minutes or until meat is tender. Stir in peas and carrots. Dissolve cornstarch in water, blend into yogurt. Stir yogurt into stew; heat. Turn stew into 2-quart casserole. Combine biscuit mix, parsley, and ⅓ cup yogurt. Spoon 6 biscuits on top of stew. Bake at 425°F 20 minutes until biscuits are browned. *Makes 6 servings*

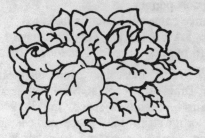

Turku Layered Casserole

½ pound ground beef
1 cup finely chopped onion
1 medium clove garlic, crushed
2 cans (15 ounces each) tomato sauce
1 teaspoon basil, crushed
½ teaspoon oregano, crushed
½ teaspoon salt
1 package (10 ounces) frozen chopped spinach, thawed and well drained
1 pint small curd cottage cheese
¼ cup grated Parmesan cheese
1 egg, slightly beaten
4 cups cooked elbow macaroni
½ pound grated **FINLANDIA Swiss Cheese**

In skillet, brown beef and cook onion with garlic until tender. Add tomato sauce and seasonings; simmer 5 minutes. Combine spinach and cottage cheese, Parmesan cheese, and egg. In 2-quart greased shallow baking dish, layer half each macaroni, grated **FINLANDIA Cheese**, and meat sauce. Cover with spinach mixture; then add remaining macaroni, grated cheese and meat sauce. Bake at 375°F. for 40 minutes, until hot and bubbly. Let stand several minutes before serving. *Makes 6 to 8 servings*

La Fiesta™ Casserole

1½ pounds ground beef
2 medium onions, chopped
½ teaspoon salt
½ teaspoon garlic salt
½ teaspoon ground cumin
¼ teaspoon pepper
2 10-ounce cans mild enchilada sauce
8 ounces **LA FIESTA™ Tortilla Strips**
2 cups (8 ounces) shredded cheddar cheese

In skillet, cook ground meat and onions till meat is brown and onion is tender. Drain off excess fat. Stir in salt, garlic salt, cumin, and pepper. Stir in enchilada sauce. In 13 × 9 × 2-inch baking dish, layer the tortilla strips, meat sauce, and cheese; repeat tortilla strips and meat layers. Cover and bake in 350° oven for 30 minutes. Uncover and sprinkle with remaining cheese. Bake 10 minutes more. *Makes 8 servings*

Chili Casserole

1 pound ground beef
½ cup chopped onion
1 tablespoon chili powder
1 teaspoon salt
¼ teaspoon oregano
1 can (30 ounces) **ROSARITA® Refried Beans**
1 can (16 ounces) stewed tomatoes
6 ounces Monterey Jack cheese
2 cups slightly broken tortilla chips

Brown beef and onion in skillet. Add chili powder, salt and oregano. Stir in beans and tomatoes. Remove from heat. Shred cheese, reserving ½ cup for topping. Spoon ½ of beef mixture into 2-quart casserole. Sprinkle with half of cheese; top with half of tortilla chips. Repeat layers. Bake at 350° for 20 minutes. Sprinkle with reserved ½ cup of cheese. Bake 5 minutes longer or until cheese has melted and mixture is bubbly. *8 servings*

Seven Layer Dinner

3 medium potatoes, sliced
2 packets **HERB-OX® Onion Flavored Instant Broth and Seasoning**
1 can (12 ounces) whole kernel corn
1 pound ground beef
½ pound fresh green beans, sliced, or 1 package (10 ounces) frozen green beans
2 medium onions, sliced
1 green pepper, slivered
1 can (1 pound) tomatoes

Fill a greased 4-quart casserole with layers of vegetables and meat in the order given, sprinkling each layer with some of the instant broth. Bake in a moderate oven (350°F.) about 2 hours.

Makes 6 servings

Monterrey Casserole

1 pound ground beef
2 tablespoons chopped onion
¾ teaspoon seasoned salt
2 8-ounce cans tomato sauce
2 cups grated Cheddar cheese
4 cups **DORITOS® Brand Taco Flavor Tortilla Chips**
½ cup ripe olives

Cook beef in skillet for 5 minutes until crumbly and light in color. Add onion, salt and tomato sauce. Simmer for 5 minutes.

Place 3 cups of **DORITOS® Brand Taco Flavor Tortilla Chips** in a 2-quart baking dish. Sprinkle 1 cup cheese over the **DORITOS® Brand Taco Flavor Tortilla Chips**.

Pour meat sauce over the above and top with remaining cheese. Garnish with remaining cup of **DORITOS® Brand Taco Flavor Tortilla Chips**.

Bake at 350° F. for 15 minutes. Top with ripe olives before serving.

Makes 4 to 6 servings

Mushroom Stroganoff Pie

1 pkg. (7½ oz.) **GOLDEN GRAIN® Stroganoff RICE-A-RONI®**
½ lb. fresh mushrooms, sliced
2 Tbsp. butter
1 lb. lean ground beef
¼ cup sour cream
1 Tbsp. chopped parsley or chives

Prepare **RICE-A-RONI®** as directed for meatless side dish. Sauté mushrooms in butter; drain liquid and stir into cooked rice. Press ground beef into bottom and sides of 10-inch pie pan; spread rice mixture over meat. Bake, uncovered, at 325°F. for 15 minutes. Cool slightly, cut into 6-8 wedges, garnish with sour cream and parsley.

Golden Meatball Casserole

1 lb. ground beef
½ cup fresh bread crumbs
1 egg
1 teaspoon salt
Oil
2 cups water
1 cup uncooked rice
2 large carrots, quartered
½ cup chopped green pepper
¼ cup chopped onion
½ lb. **VELVEETA Pasteurized Process Cheese Spread**, cubed

Combine meat, bread crumbs, egg and salt; mix lightly. Shape into 18 meatballs; brown in small amount of oil on all sides in large skillet. Drain. Add water, rice, carrots, green pepper and onion. Cover; simmer 25 minutes. Add process cheese spread; heat until process cheese spread melts.   *4 to 6 servings*

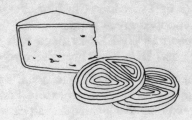

Beefy Cheese Pie

1 lb. lean ground beef
½ cup onions, finely chopped
¼ cup catsup
¼ tsp. pepper
½ cup celery, chopped
1 cup sharp Cheddar cheese, shredded
¼ cup cornflake crumbs (optional)
1 egg
¾ cup cornflake crumbs
½ tsp. garlic salt
¼ tsp. salt
2 Tbsp. margarine
1-16 oz. can **VEG-ALL**® **Mixed Vegetables**, drained

Combine ground beef, egg, onion, ¾ cup cornflake crumbs, catsup, garlic salt, pepper and salt. Press meat mixture into bottom and sides of a 9 inch pie pan. Bake in a preheated oven at 400 degrees for 15 minutes, remove from oven and drain. Reduce heat to 350 degrees.

While meat is baking, in a small skillet sauté celery in 2 Tbsp. margarine. Remove from heat and add the cheese and **VEG-ALL**® **Mixed Vegetables**. Toss lightly and spoon over top of meat. Sprinkle with the cornflake crumbs if desired. Return to oven and continue baking for about 10-15 minutes. Cut in wedges to serve.

Serves 5-6

Twisty Beef Bake

2 cups corkscrew macaroni, uncooked
1 pound ground beef
1 can (10¾ oz.) condensed cream of mushroom soup
1 can (14½ oz.) whole tomatoes, cut up
¾ cup (3 oz.) shredded Cheddar cheese
¼ cup chopped green pepper
¾ teaspoon **DURKEE Seasoned Salt**
1 can (3 oz.) **DURKEE French Fried Onions**

Cook macaroni as directed on package; drain. Brown ground beef; drain fat. Combine all ingredients except French fried onions. Pour half the mixture into a greased 2 quart casserole. Top with ½ can onions. Pour remaining macaroni mixture over onions. Cover and bake at 350° F. for 30 minutes. Uncover, top with remaining onions and bake 5 minutes longer. *Makes 4 to 6 servings*

Italian Hamburger Deep Dish

1½ pounds ground beef
1½ teaspoons salt
⅛ teaspoon pepper
1 clove garlic, finely chopped
BETTY CROCKER® POTATO BUDS® Instant
  Mashed Potatoes (enough for 8 servings)
2 tablespoons instant minced onion
1 teaspoon dried oregano leaves
3 or 4 tomatoes, sliced
4 ounces mozzarella cheese, shredded or sliced

Heat oven to 350°. Butter rectangular baking dish, 12x7½x2 inches, or 2-quart round casserole. Cook and stir ground beef, salt, pepper and garlic in 10-inch skillet until beef is brown; drain. Prepare potatoes as directed on package for 8 servings except—stir in onion and oregano. Layer half each of the potato mixture, beef mixture, tomato slices and cheese in dish; repeat. Bake uncovered 30 minutes. *6 to 8 servings*

Chinese Sliced Beef

½ cup julienne-cut carrots
½ cup diced celery (½-inch dices)
1 medium onion, sliced
1 cup frozen peas
2 teaspoons soy sauce
1 package (32 oz.) **BANQUET® Gravy and Sliced Beef Frozen Heat and Serve Buffet Supper Main Dish**
Hot rice

Place carrots, celery, and onion in boiling water for 5 minutes. Drain and place in a 2-quart oblong baking dish. Add frozen peas and soy sauce. Remove frozen gravy and sliced beef from foil tray and place into baking dish on top of vegetables. Heat in 400°F oven for 25 minutes. Separate beef slices and stir gravy and vegetables. Heat additional 15 minutes, until bubbly. Serve with hot rice. *Makes 6 servings*

Onion, Beef, Mushroom Casserole

1 pound beef
Flour
2 tablespoons fat
1 4 oz. can mushrooms
Water
Salt and pepper
¼ teaspoon Worcestershire sauce
1 can No. 303 **TAYLOR'S Whole Onions**

Dredge bite-size cubes of beef in flour; brown in fat. To liquid drained from mushrooms, add enough water to make one cup; add to beef and stir until thick and smooth. Add mushrooms and seasonings. Place onions in casserole, and top with meat mixture. Bake covered in slow oven (325°F.) two hours or until meat is tender.

Stew 'n Biscuit Bake

1 can (24 oz.) **DINTY MOORE®** **Beef Stew**
¼ cup dairy sour cream
1 cup biscuit mix
¼ cup water

In 1½ quart casserole, combine stew and sour cream. Bake in 425° F oven. Meanwhile, in small bowl, stir biscuit mix and water to make a soft dough. Drop by spoonfuls into hot stew. Bake about 20 minutes until biscuits are lightly browned.   *2 to 3 servings*

Casserole Milano

½ cup commercial sour cream
3 Tablespoons all-purpose flour
¼ cup chopped onion
2 teaspoons prepared mustard
1 can (10¾ ounces) condensed cream of celery soup,
   undiluted
2 cups cooked ham, cut into ½-inch cubes
1 package (16 ounces) **Frozen STOKELY'S®**
   Vegetables Milano®
⅓ cup dry bread crumbs
2 Tablespoons grated Parmesan cheese
2 Tablespoons butter or margarine, melted
½ teaspoon paprika

Preheat oven to 350°F. Combine sour cream, flour, onion, mustard, and soup in 2-quart casserole, blending thoroughly. Stir in ham and vegetables, spreading mixture evenly in casserole. Mix bread crumbs, cheese, butter, and paprika; sprinkle over casserole. Bake, covered, 1 hour.   *4 servings*

MICROWAVE METHOD:
Combine sour cream, flour, onion, mustard, and soup in 2½-quart covered casserole, blending thoroughly. Stir in ham and vegetables, spreading mixture evenly in casserole. Cover and microcook 15 minutes, stirring every 5 minutes (including just before topping is added). Mix bread crumbs, cheese, butter, and paprika; sprinkle over casserole and cook, uncovered, an additional 2 minutes.

Note: Use a slightly larger casserole when you make a recipe in the microwave oven. That way you will have room to stir and food will cook more evenly.

Ham Bake

1 7¼-oz. pkg. KRAFT Macaroni and Cheese Dinner
1 cup ham cubes
2 tablespoons chopped green pepper
Salt and pepper
1 cup milk
2 eggs, beaten

Prepare Dinner as directed on package. Add ham and green pepper; season to taste. Place in 10 × 6-inch baking dish. Combine milk and eggs; pour over dinner mixture. Bake at 350°, 25 to 30 minutes. *4 to 6 servings*

Treet® Hawaiian

1 12-oz. can ARMOUR STAR TREET®
4 pineapple fingers, reserving syrup
1 16-oz. can sweet potatoes, drained
¼ cup brown sugar, packed
Dash of ground cloves

Heat oven to 375°. Make 4 lengthwise slits in **ARMOUR STAR TREET®** to within ½ inch of bottom. Place one pineapple finger in each slit. Place in 1½-qt. casserole; arrange potatoes around meat. Combine ½ cup reserved pineapple syrup, brown sugar and cloves; pour over meat and potatoes. Bake at 375°, 40 minutes. To serve, cut **TREET®** and pineapple crosswise. *4 servings*

MICROWAVE METHOD:
Make 4 lengthwise slits in **ARMOUR STAR TREET®** to within ½-inch of bottom. Place one pineapple finger in each slit. Place in 1½-qt. casserole; arrange potatoes around meat. Combine ½ cup reserved syrup, brown sugar and cloves; pour over meat and potatoes. Cook, covered, 5 to 6 minutes. Let stand, covered, 5 minutes. To serve, cut **TREET®** and pineapple crosswise.

Creamettes® & Ham Casserole

7-oz. package CREAMETTES® Macaroni (2 cups uncooked)
1½ cups cubed cooked ham, or luncheon meat
1 can condensed cream of chicken soup
½ cup milk
½ cup dairy sour cream
1 package (10-oz.) frozen broccoli spears, cooked and drained
½ cup Cheddar cheese, shredded

Prepare CREAMETTES® according to package directions. Drain. Combine macaroni and ham. Pour into 13 × 9 × 2″ pan (or 3-quart casserole). Blend soup, sour cream and milk, pouring half this mixture over ham and macaroni. Arrange broccoli on top. Pour remaining sauce atop broccoli and sprinkle with cheese. Bake at 350°F. for 20 minutes.   *6 servings*

Saturday Night Supper

4 center cut pork chops, thinly sliced
1 tablespoon oil
1 28 ounce can B&M® Brick Oven Baked Beans
2 tablespoons apple jelly
2 teaspoons water
8 apple slices
Cinnamon

In a skillet, brown chops evenly in oil, about 10 minutes each side. Drain chops on paper towels. Pour beans into a 2 quart casserole and place chops on top of beans. Bake at 350°F. for 45 minutes. In a small bowl, combine jelly and water. Baste chops with this mixture and arrange apple slices on top. Sprinkle with cinnamon. Return to oven and continue baking for another 15 minutes.

Makes 4 servings

18

Country Casserole

1½ pounds ground sausage meat
6 thin slices of onion
2 cups SEALTEST® Cottage Cheese
½ teaspoon oregano
1 (7½-ounce) can tomato sauce
Sugar

Form the sausage meat into six flat cakes. Brown thoroughly on both sides over medium heat. Drain. Arrange them in an oven-proof casserole.

Place a slice of onion on each sausage cake. Mix cottage cheese with oregano. Divide equally on top of each sausage cake. Top each one with some of the tomato sauce. Sprinkle with a couple of pinches of sugar. Bake in a preheated 350° oven 25 to 30 minutes or until piping hot. *6 servings*

Tuna/Noodle Casserole
(Low Sodium)

1 can (6½ oz.) FEATHERWEIGHT® Tuna Chunks
1 can (7½ oz.) FEATHERWEIGHT® Cream of
  Mushroom Soup
2 cups cooked noodles
⅓ cup FEATHERWEIGHT® Colby or Cheddar
  Cheese, grated
¼ cup FEATHERWEIGHT® Imitation Mayonnaise
½ cup celery, chopped
¼ cup onion, chopped
2 Tbsp. green pepper, chopped
2 Tbsp. pimiento, chopped
¼ tsp. FEATHERWEIGHT® Salt Substitute
1 Tbsp. lemon juice

Combine all of the ingredients and place in a casserole dish. (Optional: Top with sliced almonds) Bake at 350°F. for 30-35 minutes. *Serves 4-5*

Approx.	Calories	Protein (Grams)	Fat (Grams)	Carbohydrate (Grams)	Sodium (Mgs.)
½ cup serving	145	8	8	11	26

Tuna Casserole

2 cans (7 oz. each) tuna, drained and flaked
2 hard cooked eggs, chopped
½ cup **BEST FOODS®/HELLMANN'S® Real Mayonnaise**
2 tablespoons chopped parsley
1 teaspoon lemon juice
½ teaspoon dry mustard
½ cup fresh bread crumbs
1 tablespoon **MAZOLA®/NUCOA® Margarine**, melted

Stir together tuna, eggs, real mayonnaise, parsley, lemon juice and mustard. Spoon into 4 individual casseroles or shells. Toss together bread crumbs and margarine. Sprinkle over tuna mixture. Bake in 375°F oven 15 minutes or until heated.

Makes 4 servings

Family Tuna Casserole

1½ cups **KELLOGG'S® 40% BRAN FLAKES Cereal**
2 teaspoons margarine or butter, melted
1 cup (4 oz.) shredded American cheese
1 can (6½ oz.) chunk light tuna in water, well-drained and flaked
1 can (10½ oz.) condensed cream of mushroom soup
⅓ cup milk
2 cups egg noodles, cooked and drained
½ cup cooked peas
½ cup thinly sliced celery
2 tablespoons chopped pimiento

1. Toss 1 cup of the **KELLOGG'S® 40% BRAN FLAKES Cereal** with the melted margarine. Set aside for topping. Set aside ½ cup of the cheese.
2. Stir together remaining cereal, remaining cheese, tuna, soup and milk. Stir in noodles, peas, celery and pimiento. Spread in 10 × 6 × 2-inch glass baking dish. Sprinkle with cereal topping.
3. Bake at 350°F for 25 minutes. Top with reserved cheese. Bake about 5 minutes longer or until cheese melts and tuna mixture is thoroughly heated.

Yield: 6 servings

Superb Swiss Tuna Bake

2 cans (6½ or 7 ounces) **STAR-KIST® Tuna**, drained
¼ cup chopped scallions
¼ pound mushrooms, chopped
½ teaspoon dried dill weed
1 teaspoon salt, divided
2 cups (8 ounces) shredded Swiss cheese, divided
6 slices bread, crusts trimmed
6 eggs
2 cups milk
1 teaspoon Worcestershire sauce
⅛ teaspoon **TABASCO® Pepper Sauce**

Flake **STAR-KIST® Tuna** in large bowl. Add scallions, mush-rooms, dill, ½ teaspoon salt, and 1 cup cheese. Mix well. Butter a shallow 2-quart baking dish. Arrange bread in baking dish. Spoon tuna mixture over bread. Beat eggs with milk, Worcestershire, **TABASCO® Sauce**, and remaining ½ teaspoon salt. Pour over tuna. Sprinkle top with remaining 1 cup cheese. Cover and chill 2 hours. Leave at room temperature ½ hour before baking. Bake in a 325° oven 1 to 1¼ hours, until tip of knife inserted in center comes out clean. (May be reheated).   *Yield: 6 servings*

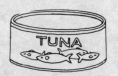

Tuna Sunflower Casserole

2 cans (7 oz. each) tuna fish, flaked
2 cans (10½ oz. each) cream of mushroom soup
⅔ cup milk
1 jar (4½ oz.) sliced mushrooms, drained
¾ cup **FISHER® Salted, Roasted Sunflower Nuts**
¼ cup chopped pimiento
½ cup crushed potato chips

Combine first 6 ingredients. Spoon into buttered 1½ quart cas-serole. Sprinkle with potato chips. Bake at 350° for 30 minutes.
Makes 4 to 5 servings

Tuna Enchiladas del Mar

1 cup oil
12 corn tortillas
30 ounces enchilada sauce
1 12½ or 13 ounce can **CHICKEN OF THE SEA®**
   Tuna, drained and flaked
1 cup scallions, minced
½ pound grated Monterey Jack cheese

Preheat oven to 350°. Place oil in skillet, heat until hot. Quickly fry 12 tortillas in oil one at a time, until soft (about 4 seconds to a side).

Remove from oil and drain on paper towels. When ready to assemble the enchiladas, dip each tortilla in enchilada sauce. Place 1 tablespoon flaked tuna in center of tortilla, add 1 generous tablespoon cheese, scallions and 2 tablespoons enchilada sauce.

Roll enchiladas and place seam side down in a greased 9 × 12 baking dish. Top with remaining enchilada sauce, sprinkle with remaining cheese and bake at 350° for 20 minutes.

Garnish with sour cream, black olives, avocado slices and tomato wedges. Serve at once.

Serves 6 (2 enchiladas per serving)

Rus-Ettes Spud-Skin Tuna Pie
(Microwave Recipe)

3 cups of frozen **RUS-ETTES Spud-Skins** or
   RUS-ETTES Rumple Spud-Skins
1 can (10¾ oz.) condensed cream of celery soup
1 can (6½ or 7 oz.) tuna, drained and flaked
¼ cup milk
¼ cup chopped green pepper
1 Tbsp. lemon juice
2 tsp. finely chopped fresh dill weed or 1 tsp. dried dill

Arrange frozen **RUS-ETTES Spud-Skins** on bottom and along sides of 1 quart shallow baking dish. Cover with plastic wrap. Microwave on high for 5 minutes. In large bowl combine soup, tuna, milk, green pepper, lemon juice, dill weed; mix well. Spoon over potatoes. Cover with plastic wrap. Microwave on high 5 minutes. Let stand 10 minutes before serving.

Yield: 4-6 servings

Tuna-Bacon Bake

7-oz. package **CREAMETTES® Macaroni** (2 cups uncooked)
¼ cup chopped onion
6 tablespoons butter or margarine
6 tablespoons flour
½ teaspoon salt
¼ teaspoon pepper
3 cups milk
1 cup process American cheese, grated
1 can (7-oz.) tuna, drained and flaked
2 tablespoons tomato catsup
1 teaspoon Worcestershire sauce
4 slices bacon
1 tomato, sliced

Prepare **CREAMETTES®** according to package directions. Drain. Sauté onion in butter until tender. Add flour, salt and pepper; cook, stirring constantly, for 2 minutes. Do not brown. Add milk; cook till smooth and thickened. Stir in cheese until melted. Combine macaroni, cheese sauce, tuna, catsup and Worcestershire. Pour into 11 × 7 × 1½" casserole and top with bacon. Bake at 350° for 15 minutes. Turn bacon and add tomato slices. Bake an additional 15 minutes.

6-8 servings

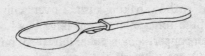

Sea Shell Casserole

1 can (6½ oz.) BUMBLE BEE® Chunk Light Tuna
1 cup shredded Cheddar cheese
¼ cup pimiento strips
8 ounces (4¼ cups) large sea shell macaroni
1 package (9 oz.) frozen cut broccoli
1 can (15 oz.) tomato sauce with tomato bits
1 teaspoon vinegar
½ teaspoon basil, crumbled
½ teaspoon salt
¼ teaspoon onion powder

Drain tuna. Combine with cheese and pimiento, and set aside.
Cook macaroni in boiling salted water as package directs, for 10
minutes. Add broccoli, and cook 4 minutes longer. Drain well.
Combine tomato sauce, vinegar, basil, salt and onion powder. Mix
with macaroni and broccoli. Turn into shallow 2-quart baking
dish. Center with tuna mixture. Cover dish. Bake in a 350°F oven
about 30 minutes, until piping hot.   *Makes 4 to 6 servings*

Impossible Seafood Pie

1 package (6 ounces) frozen crabmeat or shrimp,*
    thawed and drained
1 cup shredded process sharp American cheese (about 4
    ounces)
1 package (3 ounces) cream cheese, cut into about
    ¼-inch cubes
¼ cup sliced green onions
1 jar (2 ounces) chopped pimiento, drained, if desired
2 cups milk
1 cup **BISQUICK® Baking Mix**
4 eggs
¾ teaspoon salt
Dash of nutmeg

Heat oven to 400°. Grease pie plate, 10x1½ inches. Mix crabmeat, cheeses, onions and pimiento in plate. Beat remaining ingredients until smooth, 15 seconds in blender on high or 1 minute with hand beater. Pour into plate. Bake until knife inserted in center comes out clean, 35 to 40 minutes. Cool 5 minutes.   *6 to 8 servings*

*1 can (6 ounces) crabmeat, drained and cartilage removed, or 1 can (4½ ounces) shrimp, well rinsed and drained, can be substituted for the frozen crabmeat or shrimp.

VARIATION:

Impossible Tuna Pie

Substitute 1 can (6½ ounces) tuna, drained, for the crabmeat.

Crab & Mushroom Casserole

¼ cup butter or margarine
¼ cup chopped onion
¼ cup chopped celery
½ pound mushrooms, sliced
3 tablespoons flour
½ teaspoon salt
Dash ground ginger
2 cups **WELCH'S® White Grape Juice**
2 egg yolks, slightly beaten
1 pound crabmeat

Melt butter in large skillet. Add onion, celery and mushrooms and cook until just tender. Blend in flour, salt and ginger. Add white grape juice and cook and stir until thickened. Add a little of the hot sauce to the egg yolks, return to sauce and cook until heated through. Add and mix in crabmeat. Pour into shallow 1½ quart baking dish. Bake in 350° oven about 30 minutes.

Makes 6 servings

Broccoli Fish Casserole

10 oz. pkg. of frozen broccoli, thawed
1 to 1½ lbs. fish fillets, thawed
6 oz. **CHEEZ-OLA®**, sliced
1 teaspoon oregano
⅛ teaspoon powdered thyme
¼ cup corn oil
2 medium onions, chopped
½ green pepper, chopped
2 tablespoons flour
⅛ teaspoon pepper
1½ cups skim milk

Arrange broccoli in bottom of lightly oiled 13 × 8 × 2″ baking dish. Top with layer of fish and layer of **CHEEZ-OLA®**. Sprinkle with oregano and thyme. Heat oil on low heat and cook onions and green pepper until tender. Stir in flour and pepper. Add milk and cook, stirring constantly, until thickened. Pour over fish and **CHEEZ-OLA®** and bake at 400 degrees F. for 25 minutes or until fish flakes easily.   *Serves 4*

Scallop Casserole

1 lb. **HIGH LINER® Scallops**, thawed
4 Tbsp. butter
3 Tbsp. flour
½ tsp. salt
⅛ tsp. pepper
1 cup cream or blend
½ cup milk
1 small onion, chopped
1 medium green pepper, chopped
1 - 10 oz. can cream of mushroom soup

Melt 3 tablespoons butter in saucepan. Blend in flour and seasonings. Slowly add milk and cream, stirring constantly until thickened. Add scallops (if some are excessively large, cut in half). Simmer for 5-10 minutes, stirring occasionally. Meanwhile, sauté onion and green pepper in 1 tablespoon butter. Combine with soup. In a greased quart casserole dish, alternate layers of scallop mixture and soup mixture. Cover with buttered bread crumbs and bake in 350°F oven for 30-35 minutes. This dish is delightful served over patty shells or just by itself! *Serves 4-6*

Note: Make your casserole even more elegant by adding a can of **HIGH LINER® Lobster or Shrimp** or both!

Health Valley®
Enchiladas

2 15-ounce cans **HEALTH VALLEY® Tomato Sauce**
¾ cup water
3 teaspoons chili powder
1 clove garlic, minced
½ teaspoon tumeric
Dash of cayenne
2 15-ounce cans **HEALTH VALLEY® Spicy Vegetarian Chili With Beans**
1 12-ounce package **HEALTH VALLEY® Raw Milk Sharp Cheddar Cheese**, shredded
1 teaspoon **HEALTH VALLEY® BEST BLEND Oil**
10 **HEALTH VALLEY® Corn Tortillas**, thawed
½ cup sliced ripe olives
2 green onions, chopped

Preheat oven to 375°F. and oil an 8 × 11½-inch casserole.

In a saucepan, simmer tomato sauce, water and seasonings for 20 minutes.

Combine chili, 3 cups of cheese and ½ cup of sauce. Spoon ¼ cup sauce into prepared casserole. Soften tortillas one at a time by dipping in and out of the remaining sauce. Spoon chili-cheese mixture down center of each tortilla. Roll up and place seam side down in baking dish. Pour remaining sauce over top. Sprinkle remaining cheese, olives and green onions on top. Bake for 20 minutes in preheated oven—until hot and bubbly.

Serve with fresh avocado slices, or top the enchiladas with **HEALTH VALLEY® Avocado Dressing**.

Total Preparation Time: 45 minutes   *Yield: 5 or 6 servings*

Quickie Bean Bake

½ cup **GRANDMA'S®** **Unsulphured Molasses**
3 tablespoons vinegar
3 tablespoons prepared mustard
½ teaspoon **TABASCO®** **Pepper Sauce**
3 cans (1 pound each) baked beans in tomato sauce
1 can (1 pound) kidney beans, drained
½ pound frankfurters, cut in 1-inch pieces
1 cup diced cooked ham
1 medium onion, chopped, divided

Mix molasses, vinegar, mustard and **TABASCO®**. Add to baked beans, kidney beans, frankfurters and ham in 3-quart casserole. Add half of chopped onion; mix well. Bake in 375°F. oven 1 hour. Stir before serving. Sprinkle remaining chopped onion around edge of casserole. *Yield: 8 servings*

Note: When heating *canned* baked or kidney beans, add **GRANDMA'S®** **Unsulphured Molasses** and a little chopped onion for extra flavor.

Country Cooking Casserole

1-12 oz. can **HORMEL Sausage Patties—Hot**
1-15 oz. can **HORMEL Chili Beans in Chili Sauce**
1-15 oz. can blackeyed peas
1-17 oz. can green lima beans
1-15 oz. can golden (or white) hominy (optional) or
   substitute another choice of beans if desired
2 Tbsp. dehydrated onion flakes
1 tsp. celery seed (optional)
½ cup packed brown sugar
½ cup barbecue sauce
⅓ cup all-purpose flour

In large pan, over medium heat, thicken beans, peas and juices with flour. Add onion, celery seed, sugar and barbecue sauce. Pour into large casserole or baking dish. Lay patties on top. Bake in moderate oven (350°F) 30-35 minutes, or until hot and bubbly.

Serves 6

Tamale Pollo Casserole

1 cup finely crushed corn chips
1 15 oz. can **WOLF® Brand Tamales**
1 10 oz. can **WOLF® Brand Plain Chili**
1½ cups chopped cooked chicken
1 8 oz. can whole kernel corn, undrained
1 4 oz. can chopped can chopped green chilies, drained
1 cup (4 oz.) shredded Cheddar cheese

Sprinkle corn chips evenly onto bottom of 8-inch square baking dish. Unwrap tamales; arrange over corn chips. Combine remaining ingredients except cheese; mix well. Spoon over tamales. Bake in preheated moderate oven (350°F.) 20 minutes. Sprinkle with cheese; continue baking about 5 minutes. Serve with sour cream.

Serves 5 to 6

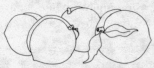

Peachy Bean Casserole

1 can (16 ounces) **VAN CAMP'S® Brown Sugar Beans**
2 Tablespoons **STOKELY'S FINEST® Tomato Catsup**
¼ cup peach preserves
2 Tablespoons chopped onion
¼ teaspoon soy sauce
4 chicken thighs or breasts

Preheat oven to 350°F. Combine beans, catsup, preserves, onion, and soy sauce in a 10 × 6 × 2-inch baking dish. To coat chicken pieces evenly with sauce, nestle chicken in bean mixture, skin side down, then turn pieces skin side up; cover and bake 1 hour. Uncover and bake an additional 30 minutes, basting chicken with sauce occasionally.

4 servings

Frankly Mexican Casserole

1 package FRENCH'S® Scalloped Potatoes
½ pound frankfurters, sliced
1 can (15-oz.) kidney beans, drained and rinsed
1 tablespoon butter or margarine
¼ cup fine dry bread crumbs
½ teaspoon FRENCH'S® Chili Powder

Prepare potatoes as directed on package, except use 2-quart casserole and increase boiling water to 2⅔ cups. Stir in frankfurters and beans. Bake in 400° oven 35 minutes; stir casserole. Melt butter in small pan; stir in bread crumbs and chili powder. Sprinkle over casserole and bake 10 to 15 minutes longer, until potatoes are tender.   *6 servings*

MICROWAVE METHOD:
Combine potato slices with 3 cups hot tap water in 2-quart casserole. Cover; cook on HIGH 14 minutes. Stir in ⅔ cup milk, seasoning mix, kidney beans, and frankfurters. Cook, covered, 7 minutes. Sprinkle with crumb mixture; cook 2 minutes.

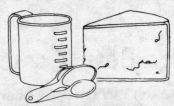

Chili and Tamale Casserole

2-15 oz. cans GEBHARDT®'S Tamales
1-15 oz. can GEBHARDT®'S Chili, with or without
   Beans
½ cup onions, chopped
1 cup grated Cheddar cheese

Drain 2 cans of tamales and remove wrappers. Place them in the bottom of a lightly greased 9 × 13″ baking dish. Cover with the chili, grated cheese and onion. Bake in a 350° F oven for 20 minutes or until hot and cheese is melted.   *Serves 4*

All-in-One Casserole

1⅓ cups water
2 tablespoons margarine or butter
½ cup milk
1⅓ cups **HUNGRY JACK® Mashed Potato Flakes**
1 lb. ground beef
½ cup chopped onion
10¾-oz. can condensed tomato soup
16-oz. can **GREEN GIANT® Cut Green Beans**, drained
¼ teaspoon oregano leaves
¼ teaspoon garlic salt
⅛ teaspoon pepper
Paprika

Heat oven to 350°F. In medium saucepan, heat water and margarine to rolling boil; remove from heat. Add milk and flakes; stir to desired consistency. Set aside. Brown ground beef and onion in large skillet; drain. Add soup, green beans, oregano, garlic salt and pepper; mix until well blended. Spoon into 1½-quart casserole; top with mashed potatoes. Sprinkle with paprika. Bake at 350°F. for 15 to 20 minutes or until thoroughly heated.

HIGH ALTITUDE—Above 3500 Feet: No change.   *4 servings*

Apple Sizz-n-Rice Casserole

12 ounce package **SIZZLEAN®**
2⅔ cups cooked rice
⅓ cup chopped onion
½ cup orange juice
1⅓ cups cubed apples
⅓ cup raisins, plumped
⅛ teaspoon cinnamon
¾ teaspoon brown sugar

Cook rice according to package directions, substituting ½ cup of orange juice for ½ cup water. Cut half of the **SIZZLEAN®** slices into 1 inch pieces. In a skillet over medium heat cook **SIZZLEAN®** pieces until well browned. Pour off all but 1 teaspoon of drippings. Cook onion in drippings until tender. Add remaining ingredients, including the rice. Mix well. Place in greased 2 quart casserole. Place whole strips of **SIZZLEAN®** over all. Bake in a 375°F. oven about 35 minutes.

Spinach Supper Ring

1 loaf **RHODES™ Frozen Honey Wheat or White Bread Dough**, thawed as directed
2 (10-oz.) packages chopped frozen spinach, thawed and very well drained
½ lb. sliced pepperoni or chopped cooked ham
1 (2½-oz.) jar sliced mushrooms, drained or ½ cup sliced fresh mushrooms
1½ cups (6 oz.) shredded mozzarella cheese
1 egg white
1 tablespoon water
2 to 3 teaspoons sesame seeds, optional

Let dough rise until nearly doubled. Preheat oven to 350°F. Roll and pat out dough to a 10 × 15-inch rectangle. Sprinkle spinach over surface. Top with pepperoni, mushrooms, and cheese.

Starting from long side, roll as for jelly roll. Pinch along seam to seal. Form a ring and pinch open ends together. Place in greased and floured 10-inch pie or cake pan or on a greased baking sheet, seam side down.

Beat egg white with water. Brush over surface of ring; sprinkle with sesame seeds. Make 5 or 6 slashes 1 to 1½ inches long on top of ring to let out steam.

Bake 30 to 40 minutes or until nicely browned. Serve hot from the oven. *Makes 6 to 8 servings*

Saucey Frank 'n Cabbage Rolls

½ pound **ECKRICH® Jumbo Beef Franks**
8 green cabbage leaves
¼ cup chopped onion
¼ cup diced fresh mushrooms
2 tablespoons chopped green pepper
2 tablespoons chopped celery
1 tablespoon butter
1 teaspoon salt
½ teaspoon garlic powder
⅛ teaspoon pepper
1½ cups cooked brown rice
1 can (10¾ ounces) tomato soup

Slice franks in half lengthwise; set aside. Cook cabbage leaves in salted water for 5 minutes; drain well. In medium skillet, cook onion, mushrooms, green pepper, and celery in butter for 3 minutes. Remove from heat and stir in seasonings and rice. Divide filling evenly between cabbage leaves. Top each with frank half; roll up. Place cabbage rolls, seam side down, in shallow baking dish. Combine tomato soup and ⅓ cup water. Pour over cabbage rolls. Bake, uncovered, at 350° for 30 minutes.   *4 servings*

Calories: 354 calories per serving.
1 serving = (2 cabbage rolls, ¼ cup sauce.)

Beefy Stuffed Cabbage

12 large cabbage leaves
1 can (16 ounces) stewed tomatoes
1 tablespoon lemon juice
1 tablespoon brown sugar
½ teaspoon **AC'CENT® Flavor Enhancer**
¼ teaspoon dry mustard
2 cans (4½ ounces each) **UNDERWOOD® Corned Beef Spread**
2 cups cooked rice
¼ cup chopped onion

Preheat oven to 350°F. In a covered saucepan, in 1 inch boiling water, cook cabbage leaves 5 minutes; drain; set aside. In a bowl, stir together tomatoes, lemon juice, brown sugar, flavor enhancer and dry mustard; set aside. In a small bowl, mix together corned beef spread, rice and onion. In center of each cabbage leaf, place portion of meat mixture. Fold 2 sides of leaf toward center; from narrow edge of leaf roll up jelly roll fashion. Place filled leaves, seam side down, in a 1½-quart shallow casserole. Spoon sauce over rolls. Bake covered 45 minutes.

Makes 4 to 6 servings

Dutch Pantry Pie

Pastry:
2 cups sifted flour
1½ tsp. salt
½ cup **WESSON®Oil**
2 Tbsp. undiluted evaporated milk
2 Tbsp. water

Mix flour and salt. Measure oil, milk and water in same cup (but don't stir). Pour all at once into flour; stir until mixed. Press into smooth ball. Cut in halves; flatten slightly. Place one half between two sheets of waxed paper, 12″ square. Roll out gently to edges of paper, (dampen table top to prevent slipping). Peel off top paper. If dough tears, mend without moistening. Lift paper and pastry by top corners. Place paper-side-up in 9″ pie pan. Peel off paper. Fit pastry into pan. Roll out top crust same way.

Filling:
4 slices American cheese (¼ lb.), cubed
1 cup undiluted evaporated milk
2 cups cooked potatoes, chopped
¼ cup chopped green onions and tops (or use dry onions)
2 Tbsp. chopped green pepper or pimiento
¼ to ½ tsp. salt
¼ tsp. pepper
1 can **SPAM® Luncheon Meat**, cubed

Heat oven to 425°F. Melt cheese in milk, stirring constantly. Mix with all remaining ingredients, except **SPAM® Luncheon Meat**. Spread in pastry-lined pan. Top with cubed **SPAM® Luncheon Meat**. Trim bottom crust. Place top crust over, gently peel off paper. Turn upper crust under lower crust and seal by pressing edges together. Flute. Make 3 or 4 slashes near center. Bake 35-40 minutes. Serve hot, with Sauce.*   *Makes 6 to 8 servings*

*Sauce

Heat together 1 can undiluted soup (mushroom, tomato, chicken or celery) and ½ cup undiluted evaporated milk.

Super Simple
Canadian Bacon Pie

2 cups cubed **COUNTRY SMOKED MEATS Canadian Bacon**
1 jar (4½ oz.) sliced mushrooms, drained
½ cup sliced green onions
½ teaspoon salt
1 cup shredded natural Swiss cheese
1½ cups milk
¾ cup packaged biscuit mix (**BISQUICK®**)
3 eggs

Heat oven to 400°. Grease pie plate, 10 × 1½ inches. Sprinkle Canadian Bacon cubes, mushrooms, onions, salt and cheese in pie plate. Beat remaining ingredients until smooth, 15 seconds in blender on high or 1 minute with hand beater. Pour into plate. Bake until knife inserted between center and edge comes out clean, 30 to 35 minutes. Cool 5 minutes.   *6 to 8 servings*

Baked Roller Coaster
Ring Around

4 eggs
2 cans (15 oz. each) **CHEF BOY-AR-DEE® Roller Coasters With Tiny Meatballs**
2 cups milk
Nutmeg
¼ cup chopped pimiento, drained
1 cup grated Cheddar cheese
3 tablespoons instant minced onion
1 medium onion, thinly sliced

Place baking pan (suitable for holding 6½ cup ring mold) with 1″ water in it, in oven. Set oven for 350°F. Beat eggs lightly. Combine with remaining ingredients, saving 6 to 8 meatballs from **Roller Coasters** for garnish. Stir gently. Pour in well-greased ring mold or spring pan. Place in water in baking pan. Bake for 55 minutes or until inserted knife comes out clean. Allow to set for 10 minutes. Unmold; garnish with onion slices and meatballs.

Serves 8

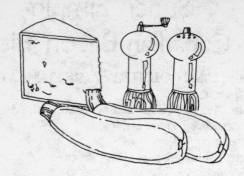

Layered Wheat Germ Supper Pie

2 frozen patty shells, thawed
6 Tbsp. **KRETSCHMER Regular Wheat Germ**,
   divided
3 cups sliced zucchini (3 medium)
½ cup chopped onion
1 small clove garlic, minced
½ tsp. dill weed
¼ tsp. salt
⅛ tsp. pepper
1 Tbsp. butter or margarine
1¼ cups grated Monterey Jack cheese
2 Tbsp. minced parsley

Press patty shells together. Roll patty shells into an 8-inch circle on cloth-covered board sprinkled with 2 tablespoons wheat germ. Turn often to coat evenly. Press pastry into a 7-inch petite pie plate. Sauté zucchini, onion, garlic and seasonings in butter for 5 minutes until vegetables are tender-crisp. Place half the vegetable mixture in pastry shell. Cover with half the cheese. Sprinkle with remaining ¼ cup wheat germ. Repeat layers of vegetable and cheese. Bake at 425° for 15-18 minutes. Sprinkle with parsley and bake 5 minutes longer. Cut into wedges.   *Makes 2-3 servings*

Note: To make 4-6 servings follow recipe above except double ingredients. Press pastry onto bottom and sides of 9-inch spring-form pan. Bake 20-22 minutes. Top with parsley and bake 5 minutes longer.

Baked Ziti and Cheese

½ pound sweet Italian sausage
1 cup sliced mushrooms
1 cup green pepper slices, cut into 2-inch lengths
⅓ cup chopped onion
½ cup butter or margarine
⅓ cup unsifted all-purpose flour
2¼ cups milk
2 cups shredded Cheddar cheese
½ cup grated Parmesan or Romano cheese
½ teaspoon each salt and pepper
3 cups (8 ounces) **SAN GIORGIO®** **Cut Ziti**, uncooked

Bake sausage at 350° for 30 minutes; cool. Slice sausage in thin pieces; set aside.

Sauté mushrooms, green pepper and onion in butter or margarine in 3-quart saucepan until tender, but not brown; remove vegetables from pan and set aside. Blend flour into butter or margarine in saucepan; gradually stir in milk. Cook and stir constantly over medium low heat until mixture begins to boil. Boil and stir 1 minute. Add 1½ cups Cheddar cheese and Parmesan or Romano cheese, salt and pepper; stir until cheese is melted and mixture is smooth. Set aside and keep warm.

Cook **Cut Ziti** according to package directions for 10 minutes; drain well. Stir cooked **Cut Ziti**, reserved sausage slices and reserved sautéed vegetables into the cheese sauce. Pour mixture into a buttered 2-quart casserole or baking dish. Sprinkle with remaining ½ cup Cheddar cheese. Cover with aluminum foil and bake at 350° for 20 minutes. Remove foil; bake about 10 to 15 minutes longer or until top is browned.   *4 to 6 servings*

Meat

Beef

Beef Sukiyaki in Wok
(Low Calorie)

1 medium onion, sliced
1 pound beef sirloin, cut in thin strips
1 teaspoon salt
¼ teaspoon pepper
1 tablespoon vinegar
½ pound fresh mushrooms, sliced
½ cup sliced celery
½ cup green pepper strips
1 (12 oz.) can **DIET SHASTA®** Lemon-Lime
3 tablespoons soy sauce
1 beef bouillon cube, crumbled
1 (16 oz.) can bean sprouts, drained
1 (4⅔ oz.) can bamboo shoots, drained
1 (8 oz.) can water chestnuts, drained and sliced

Sauté onion in large skillet until softened. Add beef strips. Cook and stir over high heat until lightly browned. Sprinkle with salt, pepper and vinegar. Add mushrooms, celery and green pepper. Cook 5 minutes. Add all remaining ingredients and simmer 5 minutes. *Serves 5 or 6*

Calories: 151 per serving

Round Steak Sizzler

¾ cup catsup
½ cup **LEA & PERRINS** Worcestershire Sauce
⅓ cup oil
1 teaspoon salt
3-pound boneless beef round steak

In a small bowl combine catsup, **LEA & PERRINS**, oil, and salt. Place steak in a snug-fitting bowl or doubled plastic bag. Pour catsup mixture over steak. Cover or fasten and refrigerate for 24 hours. Remove steak from marinade. Place on a rack over hot charcoal. Grill until done as desired, about 12 minutes on each side for medium, brushing with marinade occasionally. Or, if desired, place on a rack in a broiler pan. Place under a preheated hot broiler; follow preceding directions for cooking.

8 servings

Pepper Steak

1½ pounds beef round steak, cut ½ inch thick
¼ cup **CRISCO® Shortening**
1 can (8 ounces) tomatoes
1¼ cups water
½ cup chopped onion
1 small clove garlic, crushed
1 teaspoon salt
⅛ teaspoon pepper
2 teaspoons Worcestershire sauce
3 tablespoons Brown Roux*
2 large green peppers

Partially freeze meat and cut meat in strips 3 inches long and ¼ inch wide. In large skillet, brown meat strips in hot **CRISCO®**; drain off excess fat. Drain tomatoes, reserving liquid. Add reserved liquid, the water, onion, garlic, salt, and pepper to meat in skillet. Cover and simmer 50 to 60 minutes or till meat is tender. Uncover and stir in the Worcestershire sauce. Stir in the Brown Roux. Cook and stir till thickened and bubbly. Cut the green peppers in 2-inch long strips and add to meat along with the drained tomatoes which have been cut up. Simmer 5 minutes more. Serve over hot cooked rice. *Makes 6 servings*

*Brown Roux

Blend 1 cup **CRISCO® Shortening** and 1 cup flour till smooth. Stir in 2 tablespoons **KITCHEN BOUQUET®**. Refrigerate the mixture in a covered container till needed for gravy-making. To use the roux, combine 3 tablespoons roux for each cup of liquid (pan juices plus water) for gravy of medium thickness. Blend the roux into the liquid; cook and stir till gravy thickens and bubbles. Season gravy as desired with salt and pepper.

Steak Rolls

1½ pounds round steak, cut ½ inch thick
6 tablespoons shortening
¼ cup finely chopped onion
1½ cups day-old bread crumbs
1 cup crushed **JAYS Potato Chips**
½ cup chopped celery
½ teaspoon salt
¼ teaspoon poultry seasoning
Dash of nutmeg
1 tablespoon water
1 can condensed mushroom or tomato soup mixed with
  can of water

Remove bone from meat. Pound meat to flatten with edge of saucer or meat pounder. Cut into 4 pieces. Lightly brown onion in 3 tablespoons shortening. Add bread, chips, celery, seasonings and water. Place ¼ of the mixture on each piece of meat. Roll up and fasten with skewer or wooden pick. Flour and brown in remaining fat. Dilute soup with soup-can of water and pour over meat in skillet. Sprinkle with salt, pepper and nutmeg. Cover and simmer over low heat 1½ hours or until tender.   *4 servings*

Woodland Onion Chuck Steak

2½ to 3-pound boneless chuck steak
1 envelope **LIPTON® Onion** or **Beefy Onion Soup Mix**
1 cup sliced mushrooms
Heavy-duty aluminum foil (about 18″ × 18″)

Place steak on foil; sprinkle both sides with onion soup mix, then top with mushrooms. Wrap foil loosely around steak, sealing edges airtight with double fold. Place seam-side up on grate over hot coals, about 5 inches from heat. Grill 1 hour or until beef is tender.   *Makes about 6 servings*

Swiss Steak

½ cup sifted **E-Z-BAKE Flour**
3 teaspoons salt
½ teaspoon pepper
2 pounds round steak (1½ inches thick)
3 tablespoons fat
1 small onion, minced
2 cups tomatoes

Mix flour, salt and pepper. Pound into steak with tenderizer or potato masher. Brown in fat in heavy skillet. Add onions to tomatoes. Boil 5 minutes. Pour over steak. Bake in moderate oven (350°F.) 2 hours.

Spanish Pot Roast

3 to 4-lb. pot roast
1 8-oz. bottle **CATALINA French Dressing**
¾ cup water
8 small onions
8 small potatoes
1 cup stuffed green olive slices
2 tablespoons flour

Brown meat in ¼ cup dressing. Add remaining dressing and ½ cup water. Cover; simmer 2 hours and 15 minutes. Add onions, potatoes and olives; continue simmering 45 minutes or until meat and vegetables are tender. Remove meat and vegetables to serving platter. Gradually add remaining water to flour, stirring until well blended. Gradually add flour mixture to hot liquid in pan; cook, stirring constantly, until mixture boils and thickens. Simmer 3 minutes, stirring constantly. Serve with meat and vegetables.

6 to 8 servings

New England Boiled Dinner

3 to 3½ pound boneless beef pot roast (rump, chuck or round)
2 envelopes **LIPTON**® **Onion** or **Beef Flavor Mushroom Soup Mix**
1½ quarts water
4 medium potatoes, quartered
4 medium carrots, quartered
½ medium head cabbage, cut into wedges

In Dutch oven, add roast and **LIPTON**® **Onion Soup Mix** blended with water. Bring to a boil, then simmer covered, 2 hours. Add vegetables; continue cooking covered an additional 20 minutes or until beef and vegetables are tender.

Makes about 6 servings

Beef Stroganoff

2 tablespoons **MAZOLA**® **Corn Oil**
2½ pounds boneless beef chuck, cut into ¼-inch thick strips, ½-inch wide
½ pound mushrooms, sliced
1 cup finely chopped onion
2 cloves garlic, minced
1 can (28 oz.) plum tomatoes in juice
2 teaspoons salt
½ teaspoon pepper
⅓ cup **ARGO**®/**KINGSFORD'S**® **Corn Starch**
½ cup dry white wine
1 cup dairy sour cream
½ cup chopped parsley

In large skillet heat corn oil over medium heat. Add meat ¼ at a time; brown quickly on both sides. Remove meat. Add mushrooms, onion and garlic; sauté 5 minutes or until tender. Add tomatoes, salt and pepper. Simmer 10 minutes. Stir together corn starch and wine until smooth. Stir into tomato mixture. Stirring constantly, bring to boil over medium heat and boil 1 minute. Remove from heat. Stir in sour cream and parsley; add meat.

Makes 6 to 8 servings

Easy Stroganoff

1 pound ground beef
1 can (4 oz.) sliced mushrooms, drained
½ cup chopped onion
1 teaspoon salt
2 cups water
1 beef bouillon cube
1½ cups **MINUTE® Rice**
½ cup sour cream

Brown ground beef quickly with mushrooms, onion and salt in large skillet, stirring frequently. Stir in water and bouillon cube. Bring to a full boil. Stir in rice. Reduce heat; cover and simmer 5 minutes. Remove from heat. Stir in sour cream. Garnish with chopped parsley, if desired.   *Makes about 5 cups or 4 servings*

Colonial Pot Roast

2 Tablespoons vegetable oil
1 3-pound boneless beef chuck roast
Salt and pepper
1 can (16 ounces) **STOKELY'S FINEST® Stewed Tomatoes**
1 teaspoon sugar
1 teaspoon oregano
1 package (28 ounces) **Frozen STOKELY'S® SIZE WIZE® Vegetables Sized for Roast**
All-purpose flour (optional)

Heat oil in Dutch oven. Season meat with salt and pepper and brown on all sides over medium heat, about 15 minutes. Add tomatoes, sugar, and oregano. Cover and simmer 2½ to 3 hours. Add vegetables and continue cooking, covered, 1 hour, or until meat and vegetables are tender. Lift meat and vegetables from pan with slotted spoon. If gravy is desired, measure sauce from Dutch oven. Add 2 Tablespoons flour to each cup of drippings; blend and return to Dutch oven. Heat, stirring constantly, until thickened. Adjust seasoning. Serve with meat and vegetables.

4 to 6 servings

Italian Beef Stew
(Manzo Stufato)

3 tablespoons **PROGRESSO Olive Oil**
3 pounds beef shoulder, cut into 2-inch cubes
1 cup chopped onions
¼ pound sliced cooked ham, slivered
1 clove garlic, minced
1 can (28 oz.) **PROGRESSO Recipe-Ready Crushed Tomatoes**
2 tablespoons **PROGRESSO Wine Vinegar**
2 teaspoons basil leaves, crumbled
2 teaspoons salt
¼ teaspoon ground black pepper
1 can (14 oz.) artichoke hearts in brine, drained
1 package (10 oz.) frozen peas, thawed

In a large heavy ovenproof saucepot or a Dutch oven heat oil until hot. Add beef a few pieces at a time, brown on all sides. Remove beef from saucepot; set aside. To saucepot add onions, ham and garlic; sauté over moderate heat for 2 minutes. Add tomatoes, vinegar, basil, salt and black pepper; mix well. Return beef to pot. Cover and bake in a preheated slow oven (325 F.) until beef is fork-tender, about 2½ hours. Strain off fat. Add artichoke hearts and peas. Cover and bake 15 minutes longer. Serve with fettuccine noodles, if desired. *Yield: 8 portions*

Hungarian Goulash
(Low Calorie/Low Fat)

1½ pounds cubed lean beef
2 medium onions, sliced
1 can (1 pound) whole tomatoes
1 can (8 ounces) tomato sauce
1½ tablespoons paprika
1 packet **SWEET 'N LOW**®
Freshly ground pepper to taste
3 cups cooked (6 ounces uncooked) whole-wheat or spinach noodles
1 cup plain low-fat yogurt

In medium-size non-stick saucepan, brown beef on all sides. Remove beef and set aside. In same saucepan, cook onions until transparent. Return beef to pan and add tomatoes, tomato sauce, paprika, **SWEET 'N LOW®**, and pepper. Cover and simmer over very low heat 1 hour. Uncover slightly and let simmer 30 minutes, or until meat is tender and sauce has reduced a little. Meanwhile, prepare noodles according to package direction, omitting salt. Remove goulash from heat. Stir in yogurt. Reheat to serving temperature without boiling. Serve over hot noodles.

Per Serving (1¼ cups): Calories: 230; Fat: 5g   *6 servings*

Note: If you don't own a non-stick saucepan, you can spray your saucepan with a non-stick coating agent.

California Beef Stew

2 tablespoons salad oil
2 pounds beef, suitable for stew, cut in 1½-inch cubes
1 tablespoon **LAWRY'S® Seasoned Salt**
½ teaspoon **LAWRY'S® Seasoned Pepper**
1 bay leaf
2 cups water
1 cup dry red wine
1 bunch carrots
12 small boiling onions
3 medium zucchini
2 large tomatoes
2 tablespoons flour
¼ cup water

Heat oil in Dutch oven. Add beef cubes and brown thoroughly on all sides. Add Seasoned Salt, Seasoned Pepper and bay leaf. Stir in 2 cups water and wine. Bring to a boil, reduce heat, cover and simmer about 1 hour and 15 minutes. Meanwhile, peel carrots and cut in 2-inch lengths. Peel onions and pierce each end with a fork so they will retain their shape when cooked. Cut zucchini in about four diagonal pieces. Peel and quarter tomatoes. Combine flour and ¼ cup water. After beef has simmered 1 hour and 15 minutes, add carrots. About 10 minutes later add onions and zucchini. Continue simmering until meat and vegetables are tender, about 20 minutes. Add tomatoes and flour-water mixture. Combine carefully but thoroughly. Bring to a boil, reduce heat and simmer 2 to 3 minutes. Serve immediately.   *Makes about 6 servings*

Beef Burgundy

1½ pounds round steak, cut in 1½-inch cubes
1 cup dry red wine
1 small onion, quartered
½ pound (about 2 cups) small mushrooms
4 tablespoons **FLEISCHMANN'S® Unsalted Margarine**
3 cups sliced onion
2 cups diced carrots
¼ cup chopped parsley
2 cloves garlic, crushed
½ teaspoon ground marjoram
½ teaspoon thyme, crushed
¼ teaspoon pepper
1 bay leaf
1¼ cups water
2 tablespoons flour

Combine beef, ¾ cup wine and onion. Cover; refrigerate overnight. Drain beef cubes; set aside. Strain and reserve liquid. Sauté mushrooms in 3 tablespoons margarine until lightly browned; remove and set aside. Add beef; cook until well browned. Remove and set aside. Sauté sliced onion, carrots, parsley and garlic in remaining 1 tablespoon margarine until onions are tender. Add meat, marjoram, thyme, pepper, bay leaf, marinade and 1 cup water. Cover and simmer 2 hours, or until meat is tender. Dissolve flour in remaining ¼ cup water; add to beef mixture. Add mushroom and cook until mixture thickens, about 5 minutes. Stir in remaining wine.   *Makes 6 servings*

Spanish Stuffed Peppers

3 green bell peppers
1 pound lean ground beef
3 Tablespoons chopped onion
1 can (15 ounces) **VAN CAMP'S® Spanish Rice**
2 Tablespoons **STOKELY'S FINEST® Tomato Catsup**
Parmesan cheese

Preheat oven to 350°F. Cut peppers in half lengthwise; discard seeds and pith. Steam 5 minutes in covered pan with 1 inch of water; cool quickly. Meanwhile, brown ground beef and onion in skillet; drain excess fat. Stir in Spanish rice and catsup. Spoon beef mixture into pepper halves. Place filled peppers upright in 12 × 8-inch baking dish. Bake 25 to 30 minutes. Sprinkle with Parmesan cheese and serve immediately.   *6 pepper halves*

MICROWAVE METHOD:
Cut peppers in half lengthwise; discard seeds and pith. Place, cut side up, in 12 × 8-inch baking dish. Cover with waxed paper and microcook 7 minutes, turning dish once; set aside. Crumble ground beef in 1½-quart casserole; stir in onion. Microcook, covered, 4 minutes, stirring once; drain excess fat. Stir in Spanish rice and catsup. Spoon beef mixture into pepper halves. Cover with waxed paper and microcook 12 minutes, turning dish twice. Sprinkle with Parmesan cheese and serve immediately.

Sauerbraten Meatballs

1 pound lean ground round
¼ cup soft-coarse **HI HO CRACKER® Crumbs**
¼ cup minced onion
Freshly ground black pepper
2 tablespoons water
7 tablespoons lemon juice
2 tablespoons margarine
2½ cups beef broth
¼ cup brown sugar
¾ cup **SUNSHINE® Gingersnap Crumbs**

Combine meat, cracker crumbs, onion, pepper, 2 tablespoons of water and 3 tablespoons lemon juice. Mix well and form into 1-inch balls. In a skillet, heat margarine and brown meatballs. Remove from pan. To the drippings in the pan, add broth and remaining lemon juice. Bring to a boil and stir in sugar and gingersnap crumbs. Add meatballs to the sauce and simmer covered for 10 minutes. Stir and cook uncovered 5 minutes longer. Serve over noodles and sprinkle with poppy seeds.

Yield: 6 servings

Land O' Lakes Cornbread Mexi-Casserole

1 lb. ground beef
⅓ cup chopped onion
⅓ cup chopped green pepper
16-oz. can kidney beans, undrained
15-oz. can tomato sauce
½ cup sliced (⅛") ripe olives
1 Tbsp. sugar
2 tsp. chili powder
1 tsp. salt
¼ tsp. garlic powder

Cornbread Topping:

2 cups (8-oz.) shredded **LAND O LAKES® Process American Cheese** (reserve 1 cup)
½ cup yellow cornmeal
½ cup all-purpose flour
2 tsp. baking powder
¼ tsp. salt
⅔ cup milk
1 egg
2 Tbsp. **LAND O LAKES® Sweet Cream Butter**, softened

Preheat Oven: 425°F. In heavy 10″ skillet brown ground beef with onion and green pepper; drain well. Stir in kidney beans, tomato sauce, olives and seasonings. Cook, covered, over med. heat for 15 min. Meanwhile, prepare cornbread topping.*

*CORNBREAD TOPPING:

In med. bowl combine 1 cup cheese (reserve remaining 1 cup cheese) and remaining ingredients; stir to combine.

Pour ground beef mixture into 12 × 8″ baking dish; top with dollops of cornbread topping, spreading to edges. Bake near center of 425° oven for 20 to 25 min. or until cornbread topping is golden brown. Remove from oven and sprinkle with remaining 1 cup cheese.   *Yield: 6 (1 cup) servings*

Krispy® American Chopped Suey

½ pound ground lean beef
2 tablespoons shortening
⅓ cup diced onion
½ cup diced celery
1 (10½ ounce) can tomato puree
1 (8 ounce) can spaghetti sauce
2½ cups coarsely crushed **SUNSHINE® KRISPY®
  Saltine Crackers**
1 egg, beaten
1 cup grated American cheese
1 cup milk
2 tablespoons minced parsley
1 teaspoon salt

Heat oven to 325°F. Brown beef in shortening, breaking it with a spoon into small bits. Add onion, celery, tomato puree and spaghetti sauce. Cook, uncovered, over low heat for 20 minutes. Combine crushed cracker crumbs, beaten egg, grated cheese, milk, parsley and salt. Stir **KRISPY® Cracker** crumb mixture into tomato mixture. Pour into a greased 1½-quart baking dish. Bake, uncovered, at 325°F. for 40 minutes.

Yield: 4 to 5 generous servings

Oven Easy Meatballs

1½ lbs. ground beef
½ cup soft bread crumbs
1 egg
½ tsp. salt
1 can **HUNT'S® Manwich Sauce**
¼ cup water

Combine first 4 ingredients with ⅓ cup **Manwich**; form into 1-inch balls. Arrange in shallow baking pan; bake at 450° for 15 minutes. Drain excess fat. Pour remaining **Manwich** mixed with water over meatballs; bake 15 minutes longer. Turn and baste often. *Makes 6 servings*

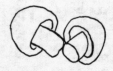

Meatball Stroganoff

1¾ cups water, divided
1 envelope (about 1.3 oz.) onion soup mix, dry, divided
4½ teaspoons Worcestershire sauce
¾ teaspoon salt, divided
1 pound ground beef
¾ cup **Instant** or **Regular RALSTON®**
1 can (4 oz.) mushroom stems and pieces, undrained
⅓ cup all-purpose flour
1 container (8 oz.) dairy sour cream
¼ cup snipped parsley

Combine ½ cup water, ½ envelope (about 3 tablespoons) soup mix, Worcestershire sauce and ½ teaspoon salt. Stir in ground beef and **RALSTON®**. Mix thoroughly. Shape into 24 balls (use about 2 tablespoons mixture for each). Place on sided baking sheet. Bake in 400° oven about 20 minutes or until done. Turn midway. Drain on absorbent paper. Meanwhile, in large saucepan combine ¾ cup water, remaining ½ envelope soup mix and undrained mushrooms.

Bring to boil. Cover. Reduce heat and simmer 5 minutes. Mix together remaining ½ cup water, flour and remaining ¼ teaspoon salt. Slowly stir into hot mixture. Heat until boiling and thickened, stirring frequently. Stir in sour cream until blended. Add parsley and meatballs. Heat thoroughly. Serve over noodles, linguini or rice.   *Makes 4-5 servings*

Rio Grande Chili

2 tablespoons salad oil
1 medium onion, chopped
1 clove garlic, crushed
1 pound ground beef
2 teaspoons salt
1 teaspoon paprika
2 teaspoons chili powder
2 cans (1 pound each) kidney beans
½ cup bean liquid
1 can (1 pound) seasoned stewed tomatoes
1 can (6 ounces) tomato paste
½ teaspoon sugar
¾ teaspoon **TABASCO® Pepper Sauce**
1 can (12 ounces) whole kernel corn, drained

Heat oil in large skillet; add onion and garlic and cook until yellow, but not brown. Add ground beef; sprinkle with salt, paprika and chili powder. Cook meat until brown, breaking up with a fork. Drain kidney beans and discard all but ½ cup liquid; reserve beans. Stir in bean liquid, tomatoes, tomato paste, sugar and **TABASCO®**. Cover and simmer 30 minutes. Add kidney beans and corn; simmer 15 minutes longer, stirring occasionally. Serve with rice if desired, and a bottle of **TABASCO® Sauce** on the side.   *Yield: About 6 servings*

Chilly Day Chili

2 medium onions, chopped
1 green pepper, coarsely diced
1 tablespoon salad oil
2 pounds lean ground beef
1 can (1 pound) tomatoes
1 can (15 ounces) tomato sauce
½ cup **HEINZ Tomato Ketchup**
1 tablespoon chili powder
2 teaspoons salt
¼ teaspoon pepper
2 cans (15½ ounces each) kidney beans, partially drained

In large kettle or Dutch oven, sauté onions and green pepper in oil until tender. Add beef stirring lightly to break up. Cover; simmer about 30 minutes or until meat loses color. Drain excess fat. Add tomatoes and next 5 ingredients. Simmer, uncovered, 30 minutes, stirring occasionally. Add kidney beans; simmer an additional 15 minutes.   *Makes 10-12 servings (about 2½ quarts)*

Note: Recipe is a mild flavored chili. Additional chili powder may be added for a spicier dish.

Glazed Meat Loaf

Meat Loaf:
1½ pounds ground beef chuck
1 cup **NABISCO 100% Bran Cereal**
½ cup chopped onion
⅓ cup ketchup
¼ cup water
2 eggs
1½ teaspoons Worcestershire sauce
1¼ teaspoons salt
¼ teaspoon ground black pepper

Glaze:
1 tablespoon ketchup
1 tablespoon dark corn syrup
¼ teaspoon Worcestershire sauce

Make meat loaf. Combine ground chuck, **NABISCO 100% Bran Cereal**, onion, ketchup, water, eggs, Worcestershire sauce, salt and pepper; mix lightly until well blended. Shape into a loaf. Place in an aluminum foil-lined 13 × 9 × 2-inch baking pan. Bake at 375°F. for 50 minutes.

Make glaze. In small bowl, blend ketchup, corn syrup and Worcestershire sauce. Brush over top of meat loaf; bake 10 minutes longer or until done.

Garnish meat loaf with parsley sprigs and surround with sautéed carrots, onions and mushrooms, which have been tossed with chopped parsley.   *Serves 6*

Zesty Saltine Meatloaf

1½ pounds ground beef
1 cup coarse **KEEBLER® ZESTA® Saltine Crackers**
⅓ cup chopped onion
¼ cup milk
1 egg
¼ cup ketchup
1 teaspoon Worcestershire sauce
1 teaspoon salt
¼ teaspoon pepper
1 cup shredded Cheddar cheese

In large mixing bowl, combine ground beef, ½ cup cracker crumbs, onion, milk, egg, ¼ cup ketchup, Worcestershire sauce, salt and pepper; blend thoroughly. Place mixture on large piece of waxed paper. Cover with another piece of waxed paper and roll out to rectangle about 9 × 15 inches. Remove top sheet of paper. Combine remaining cracker crumbs and cheese. Sprinkle over meat mixture. Beginning with 9-inch side, roll up jelly roll fashion, using waxed paper to help roll. Place in 9 × 5 inch loaf pan. Spread additional ketchup over top. Bake in preheated 350°F. oven 1-1¼ hours.   *5 to 6 servings*

Beef and Sausage Loaf

½ cup chopped onion
2 tablespoons chopped green pepper
2 tablespoons butter or margarine
2 beaten eggs
⅓ cup tomato juice
½ cup quick-cooking rolled oats
1 teaspoon salt
¼ teaspoon dry mustard
1½ pounds ground beef
½ pound **TENNESSEE PRIDE®** **Country Sausage**

Cook onion and green pepper in butter until tender but not brown. Combine eggs with next 4 ingredients and cooked vegetables. Add beef and sausage and mix well. Pat mixture into 8½ × 4½ × 2½-inch loaf dish. Bake at 350° for 1½ hours. Remove from oven and pour off excess fat. Let meat stand in pan several minutes before slicing. *Makes 8 servings*

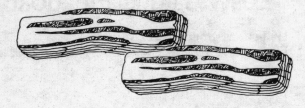

Mary Meatloaf

2 lbs. ground beef
1 package onion soup mix
2 tablespoons finely chopped onion
1½ cups **MR. & MRS. "T"®** **Bloody Mary Mix**
Bacon slices

Mix meat, onion soup mix, onion and one cup **MR. & MRS. "T"®** **Bloody Mary Mix**. Shape into loaf shape. Place in baking pan. Top with bacon slices. Bake in preheated 350° oven for 45 minutes. Drain off fat. Add remaining **MR. & MRS. "T"®** **Bloody Mary Mix** to pan. Baste loaf. Thicken pan juices slightly with a little cornstarch mixed with water. Serve meatloaf with green salad. *Serves 4-6*

Mighty Mini Meat Muffins

2 eggs beaten
1 cup rolled crumbs of **BROWNBERRY® Natural Wheat Bread**
1 lb. ground beef
2 Tbsp. steak sauce
1 tsp. salt
¾ cup milk

Preheat oven to 450°. Mix ingredients in order given and pack mixture level or slightly rounded into greased muffin tins. Bake 15 minutes.   *Makes 6 servings*

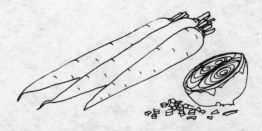

Corned Beef and Cabbage

1 4-pound corned beef
Cold water
½ bottle **SOUVERAIN White Wine**
¼ teaspoon peppercorns
¼ teaspoon bay leaves
½ teaspoon parsley
1 medium size onion, chopped
1 large carrot, sliced
1 can of small white potatoes
1 2-pound cabbage, cut in quarters

Wash corned beef thoroughly. Put it into a large pot and cover with equal parts of water and **SOUVERAIN White Wine.** Add all other ingredients except cabbage. Simmer very gently for 3 hours. Skim when a scum rises. Wash cabbage well, add to pot and simmer for a further 20 minutes, or until the cabbage is cooked.   *Serves six*

Corned Beef With Vegetables

SWIFT PREMIUM® Corned Beef for Oven Roasting
1 cup water
1 medium head cabbage, cut into 6 wedges
3 medium carrots, pared
3 onions, peeled
3 potatoes, pared and cut into halves
½ cup water

Place meat on a rack in a large Dutch oven. Add 1 cup water. Cover. Place in a 325°F. oven for 2½ hours. Arrange vegetables around meat. Add ½ cup water. Cover and continue cooking 30 minutes or until meat and vegetables are tender. *Yield: 6 servings*

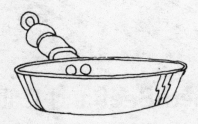

Skillet Barbecued Corned Beef

1 can (12 oz.) **LIBBY'S® Corned Beef**
1 cup shredded carrots, lightly packed
1 jar (12 oz.) chili sauce
1½ teaspoons Worcestershire sauce
6 toasted hamburger buns
Midget gherkins and carrot curls, garnish

Crumble corned beef into a heavy skillet. Add carrots, chili sauce and Worcestershire sauce; stir to mix well. Heat until bubbly. Reduce heat and cover; simmer, stirring occasionally, for 30 minutes. Serve on toasted hamburger buns. Garnish each with a midget gherkin tucked inside a carrot curl if desired.

Yields 6 sandwiches

Veal

Continental Veal Cutlets

2 cups fresh bread crumbs
¾ teaspoon *each* oregano, basil, and garlic salt
1 lb. Italian-style veal cutlets
2 eggs, lightly beaten
Oil for frying
1 can (7 oz.) **ORTEGA Green Chile Salsa**
¼ cup grated Parmesan cheese

Combine bread crumbs, oregano, basil and garlic salt. Dip veal cutlets in eggs. Coat egg-covered cutlets with seasoned crumbs; quickly sauté in skillet in oil until golden brown on both sides. Lay cutlets in shallow baking pan. Pour salsa over cutlets and top with cheese. Bake in preheated oven (350°) for 15-20 minutes, or until heated through. Do not overcook.   *Serves 4-6*

Veal Cutlet Parmesan

1 lb. veal cutlets
½ lb. Mozzarella cheese
1 cup dry breadcrumbs
2 beaten eggs
1 can tomato sauce
1 tsp. salt
Dash of pepper

Dip cutlets in beaten eggs combined with seasoning, then breadcrumbs. Fry in **FILIPPO BERIO Olive Oil** until brown (about 8 minutes). Then place cutlets in baking dish, spread tomato sauce and slices of mozzarella cheese over them.

Bake in moderate oven 10 to 15 mins.   *Serves 4*

Pork

Peachy Pork Chops

6 loin pork chops, 1-inch thick
1 Tbsp. butter or oil
½ cup chopped onion
½ cup chopped green pepper
1 can (16 oz.) **DEL MONTE Lite Peach Halves**
1 cup beef broth
1½ tsp. thyme
1 tsp. dry mustard
¼ tsp. garlic powder
Dash salt
Dash pepper
6 green pepper rings (sliced crosswise)

In skillet, brown meat in butter and remove from pan. Sauté onion and pepper. Drain fruit reserving ½ cup liquid. Return meat to pan; add broth, reserved liquid, thyme, mustard, garlic powder, salt and pepper. Cover and simmer 45 minutes. Garnish each chop with peach half and pepper ring. Sprinkle with chopped parsley, if desired.   *6 servings*

Sweet Sour Pork Chops

6 rib pork chops, ½-inch thick
1 tablespoon shortening
Salt and pepper
½ cup **HEINZ Tomato Ketchup**
½ cup pineapple juice
1 tablespoon brown sugar
1 tablespoon lemon juice
2 tablespoons minced onion
1 teaspoon **HEINZ Worcestershire Sauce**
½ teaspoon salt
⅛ teaspoon ground cloves

Brown chops in shortening; drain excess fat. Sprinkle lightly with salt and pepper. Combine ketchup and remaining ingredients; pour over chops. Cover; simmer 45 minutes, basting occasionally, or until meat is tender. Skim excess fat from sauce.

Makes 6 servings (about 1 cup sauce)

Orange Spiced Pork Chops

6 pork chops, 1-2 inches thick
⅓ cup **DOMINO® Liquid Brown Sugar**
½ cup water
3 tablespoons frozen orange juice concentrate, thawed
1 teaspoon dry mustard
¼ teaspoon ground ginger
1 orange, sliced

Preheat oven to 375°F. Place pork chops in large shallow baking dish, 13 × 9-inch. To make sauce, combine **DOMINO® Liquid Brown Sugar**, water, orange juice concentrate, mustard and ginger. Pour over pork chops. Bake 20 minutes. Turn chops and baste with sauce. Bake 25 minutes. Top with orange slices, brush with sauce and bake 15 minutes longer or until chops are tender. To serve, place chops on warmed platter. Spoon over sauce. Garnish with orange slices.

Makes 6 servings

Western Pork Chops

2 tablespoons **MAZOLA®/NUCOA®** **Margarine**
4 shoulder or center pork chops (about 1½ lbs.)
1 cup chopped green pepper
1 cup chopped onion
1 can (8 oz.) tomato sauce
½ cup **KARO® Light** or **Dark Corn Syrup**
¾ teaspoon chili powder

In medium skillet melt margarine over medium heat. Add pork chops; cook until brown on all sides, about 10 minutes. Remove chops from skillet. Add peppers and onion; cook until tender, about 5 minutes. Stir tomato sauce, corn syrup and chili powder into skillet; add chops. Simmer, uncovered, about 30 minutes or until pork chops are tender. If desired, serve over cooked noodles and garnish with parsley.

Makes 4 servings

Easy Pork Chops
and Rice Bake

5 pork chops, ½ inch thick
1 tablespoon cooking oil
1 cup **UNCLE BEN'S® CONVERTED® Brand Rice**
1 can (10½ ounces) beef broth
1 cup sliced carrots
½ cup chopped onion
2 tablespoons steak sauce
1 tablespoon salt
¼ teaspoon pepper
½ teaspoon basil

Brown pork chops in oil. In a 2-quart baking dish (12″ × 8″ × 2″)
add rice, beef broth, one soup can of water, carrots, onions, steak
sauce, salt, pepper and basil. Arrange pork chops over rice mixture. Cover and bake in 350°F. oven 45 minutes. Uncover and
continue baking 10 minutes more or until all water is absorbed.

Makes 5 servings

Pork Tenderloins in
Sour Cream Sauce

1-2 lb. **FARMLAND CUSTOM CUT**™ **Pork
  Tenderloin**, sliced ½″ thick
¾ teaspoon dried sage, crushed
½ teaspoon salt
Dash pepper
2 tablespoons shortening
1 medium onion, sliced
1 beef bouillon cube
¼ cup boiling water
1 cup sour cream
1 tablespoon all-purpose flour

Slice meat and rub with a mixture of sage, salt, and dash pepper. Brown lightly on both sides in hot shortening. Drain off excess fat; add onions. Dissolve bouillon cube in ¼ cup boiling water. Pour over meat. Cover and simmer 30 minutes or until meat is done. Remove meat. Prepare gravy by combining sour cream and flour in small bowl. Slowly stir in meat drippings. Return mixture to skillet; cook and stir just until boiling. Add water until gravy is desired consistency. Place meat on noodles and spoon on gravy.

Serves 4 to 6

Orange Glazed
Smoked Pork

½ cup firmly packed brown sugar
2 tablespoons **ARGO®/KINGSFORD'S® Corn Starch**
¼ teaspoon ground cinnamon
¼ teaspoon ground cloves
3 cups orange juice
1 (2 lb.) smoked pork shoulder roll (butt)
6 small sweet potatoes (about 1½ lb.), pared, halved
1 package (11 oz.) mixed dried fruit (2 cups)

In 2-quart saucepan stir together sugar, corn starch, cinnamon and cloves until well mixed. Gradually stir in juice until smooth. Stirring constantly, bring to boil over medium heat and boil 1 minute. In 13 × 9 × 2-inch baking pan place pork, potatoes and fruit. Spoon orange sauce over all. Bake in 325°F oven, basting frequently, 2 hours or until temperature on meat thermometer reaches 170°F and potatoes are tender. *Makes 6 servings*

Pork and Sauerkraut Sensation

Two 1 lb. cans sauerkraut
2 tablespoons bacon drippings or oil
1 large onion, chopped
1 apple, chopped
6 peppercorns
1 cup chicken broth
1 cup dry white wine or water
6 **WILSON®** Smoked Pork Loin Chops
1 lb. **WILSON®** Smoked, **Beef** or **Polish** Sausage

Rinse sauerkraut and drain. Place bacon drippings in Dutch oven or large skillet with a lid. Add onion and sauté until tender. Add drained sauerkraut, apple, peppercorns, chicken broth and wine or water. Cover and simmer 1 hour. Nestle chops into sauerkraut around the edges. Lightly score sausage. Place on top of sauerkraut. Cover and simmer ½ hour. Serve this sauerkraut dish with boiled potatoes and spicy mustard. *Makes 6 servings*

Ham Tahiti

HORMEL CUREMASTER® Ham (about 2 lbs.)
Fresh pineapple slices, trimmed of rind
¼ cup butter
¼ Tbsp. cornstarch
1 cup pineapple juice
1 tsp. curry powder
1 Tbsp. chutney

Cut 5 slices half-way into ham, bake as directed. For glaze melt butter in a small saucepan, blend in cornstarch, pineapple juice, curry powder and chutney. Cook and stir until thickened. After 25 minutes of baking, insert half slices of pineapple into cuts in ham. Glaze and continue baking and glazing. To serve, arrange ham on platter with pineapple top.

Ham & Potato Skillet Feast

1-12 oz. can **HORMEL Ham Patties** (Cut into halves)
2 Tbsp. margarine or butter
1 pkg. **BETTY CROCKER® Scalloped Potatoes**
2 medium carrots (sliced)
2¾ cups water
⅔ cup milk
½ tsp. dried basil leaves (crushed)
¼ tsp. garlic salt
⅛ tsp. pepper
1 small zucchini (thinly sliced)
1 medium tomato (chopped)

Cook ham patties in margarine in 10-inch skillet until light brown. Remove ham patties; stir in potatoes, Sauce Mix, carrots, water, milk, basil, garlic salt and pepper. Heat to boiling, stirring frequently; reduce heat. Cover and simmer, stirring occasionally, 20 minutes. Stir in zucchini and tomato; top with ham patties. Cover and cook 10 minutes longer.   *6 servings*

Very Merry Ham

1 can (5 lb.) **RATH® Hickory Smoked Ham**
1 cup apricot preserves
2 egg yolks, slightly beaten
Maraschino cherry halves
Pecan halves

Heat ham on wire rack as directed on can. Last 20 minutes of heating time, remove ham from oven; increase temperature to 350°F. Score fat surface of ham in diamond pattern. Put 1 cherry or pecan half in center of each diamond. Combine preserves and egg yolks. Carefully spoon over decorated top and spread on sides of ham. Heat ham 15 minutes more. (Do not baste.)

Makes 14 4-oz. servings

Hamballs With Pineapple Sauce

Hamballs:

24 ounces **OSCAR MAYER Ham**, ground
8 ounces lean ground pork
1 cup soft bread crumbs
¼ cup finely chopped onion
2 eggs, slightly beaten
½ cup milk

Sauce:

1 can (8½ oz.) crushed pineapple
½ cup firmly packed brown sugar
1 tsp. cornstarch
⅓ cup catsup
⅓ cup vinegar
2 Tbsp. soy sauce
½ tsp. ginger

3 cups hot cooked rice

Preheat oven to 350°. Combine hamball ingredients in bowl; mix well. Shape into 2-inch balls and place in a 9 x 13 inch shallow baking pan. To make sauce, empty can of crushed pineapple into bowl. Mix brown sugar with cornstarch; add to pineapple. Stir in remaining ingredients. Pour sauce over hamballs and bake 50 minutes. Serve over hot cooked rice.

Makes about 18. Allow 3 per serving

Note: These can be made into 1-inch appetizer balls as well.

Ham Waikiki

1 can (1 lb. 4 oz.) pineapple slices
1 tablespoon cornstarch
1 tablespoon **LEA & PERRINS Worcestershire Sauce**
1 teaspoon ground ginger
3-pound ready-to-eat ham steak

Drain pineapple; set aside slices and juice separately. In a small saucepan combine cornstarch with **LEA & PERRINS** and ginger. Blend in reserved pineapple juice (about 1 cup). Cook and stir over moderate heat until thickened. Place ham on a rack in a broiler pan. Brush pineapple juice mixture over ham. Place under a preheated hot broiler for 10 minutes, brushing once more. Turn ham. Add reserved pineapple slices to broiler rack. Brush ham and pineapple slices with pineapple juice mixture. Broil until ham and pineapple are well glazed, about 10 minutes, brushing once more.

8 to 10 servings

Glazed Cantonese Ham Patties

¾ lb. ground ham
¼ lb. lean ground pork
¾ cup soft bread crumbs
¼ cup chopped onion
2 tablespoons chopped green pepper
½ cup **LA CHOY® Water Chestnuts**, chopped
½ teaspoon dry mustard
1½ teaspoons **LA CHOY® Soy Sauce**
1½ teaspoons prepared horseradish
2 tablespoons **LA CHOY® Sweet & Sour Sauce**
½ cup buttermilk
1 egg beaten
Additional **LA CHOY® Sweet & Sour Sauce**
Pimiento strips

Combine ham, pork, bread crumbs, onion, green pepper, water chestnuts, dry mustard, soy sauce, horseradish, and Sweet & Sour Sauce. Add buttermilk and egg; mix lightly. Shape into eight patties. Bake at 350 degrees for 25 minutes. Brush tops lightly with additional Sweet & Sour Sauce; bake 5 minutes more. Garnish with pimiento strips.

8 servings

Ham 'n Sweets Skillet Dinner

¼ cup finely chopped onion
¼ cup butter or margarine
2 tablespoons flour
1 15¼-oz. can pineapple chunks, drained, reserving
  syrup
⅓ cup water
⅓ cup brown sugar, packed
1 29-oz. can sweet potatoes, drained, sliced
5 **ARMOUR® STAR Ham Patties**

Cook onion in butter or margarine 2 to 3 minutes; stir in flour. Add reserved syrup and water; cook, stirring constantly, until thickened. Stir in pineapple and brown sugar. Top with sweet potatoes and ham patties. Cook, covered, 20 to 25 minutes or until heated through. Preparation time: 35 minutes   *5 servings*

Creamed Ham and Asparagus in Parmesan Puff Ring

2 tablespoons butter or margarine
¼ cup finely chopped onion
2 tablespoons flour
½ teaspoon salt
¼ teaspoon pepper
1 cup milk
½ cup cream
½ cup shredded Swiss cheese
2 tablespoons grated Parmesan cheese
2 cups ½" cubes **WILSON® Ham**
1¼ cups 1" pieces cooked fresh or frozen asparagus

Melt butter in medium saucepan. Add onion and sauté until tender. Stir in flour, salt and pepper until thoroughly blended. Add milk and cream. Cook over medium heat, stirring constantly, until mixture thickens and comes to a full boil. Stir and boil 1 minute. Reduce heat. Stir in cheeses, until melted. Stir in ham and asparagus. Cook until ham is heated. Serve over toast, biscuits or in Parmesan Puff Ring*.   *Makes 4 to 6 servings*

*Parmesan Puff Ring

¾ cup water
6 tablespoons butter
¾ cup flour
½ teaspoon salt
3 eggs
¼ cup grated Parmesan cheese

Heat oven to 400°F. Bring water and butter to a full boil in a medium saucepan over medium heat. Add flour and salt all at once. Stir vigorously until mixture forms a ball and leaves the sides of the pan. Add eggs, one at a time, beating well after each addition. After adding the last egg, stir vigorously 1 minute. Stir in 3 tablespoons Parmesan cheese. Butter a 9″ pie pan or shallow casserole. Spoon dough in a ring around the bottom of the pan, leaving the center open. Sprinkle with remaining 1 tablespoon Parmesan cheese. Bake 35 minutes or until lightly browned. Serve as a bread or fill center with Creamed Ham and Asparagus.

Makes 6 servings

Slavic Ham Kabobs

3 pounds cooked **ATALANTA/KRAKUS/POLKA Polish Ham**, cut into 1-inch cubes
3 apples, cut in wedges
6 apricots, halved and seeded
3 green bananas, cut into 1½ inch pieces
1 jar (10 ounces) grape jam
2 tablespoons honey
¼ teaspoon curry powder
⅛ teaspoon ground ginger

Arrange ham, apples, apricots and bananas on skewers. In a small saucepan, combine jam, honey, curry and ginger. Heat, stirring, until jam is melted and sauce is heated. Grill kabobs 3 to 5 inches from heat, basting with grape sauce. Turn and baste several times until heated through. Serve hot on cooked rice.

Makes 6 servings

Note: For classic ham kabobs alternate cherry tomatoes, mushroom caps and green pepper squares with cubes of ham.

Mock Bacon Filets

4 slices **JOHN MORRELL®** **Bacon**, partially cooked
2 lbs. ground beef
¼ cup chopped green pepper
¼ cup chopped onion
½ cup chili sauce
1 teaspoon Worcestershire sauce
1 teaspoon sweet basil
½ teaspoon salt
⅛ teaspoon black pepper
2 cups sliced fresh mushrooms
2 tablespoons butter or margarine
Wooden picks
Savory Tomato Sauce*

Combine beef, pepper, onion, chili and Worcestershire sauces, basil, salt and pepper in bowl; mix well. Form mixture into 8 patties; set aside. In small skillet, sauté mushrooms in butter over low heat until soft; drain. Spoon small amount of mushrooms on center of four patties; cover each with remaining four patties and seal edges. Wrap bacon slice around each filet; secure with pick. Place on rack in shallow pan; spoon Savory Tomato Sauce over each patty. Bake in preheated 350° oven, 45 minutes. Garnish with sautéed whole mushrooms.   *Yield: 4 servings*

*Savory Tomato Sauce

8 oz. can tomato sauce
6 oz. can tomato paste
½ teaspoon Worcestershire sauce
½ teaspoon sweet basil
½ teaspoon parsley
4 drops hot red pepper sauce
Pinch garlic salt
Pinch thyme

Combine all ingredients in bowl; mix well.   *Yield: 1¼ cups*

Lamb

Savory Roast Lamb

1 leg of lamb (6 to 7 lbs.)
2 thin slices of ham
1 teaspoon salt
1 tablespoon minced parsley
1 peppercorn
1 to 2 garlic cloves
2 tablespoons **POMPEIAN Olive Oil**

Combine salt, parsley, peppercorn and garlic; mash to a paste. Blend in **POMPEIAN Olive Oil**. Spread this mixture over the ham. Cut ham into thin slivers. Force deep gashes in lamb with sharp thin knife; force ham strips into the holes. Brush meat all over with additional **POMPEIAN Olive Oil** and roast at 325° until meat thermometer registers 150° (pink), about 25 minutes to the pound for medium well done. *Serves 6*

Mexicana Lamb

4-5 lbs. lamb, cut into 1½″ cubes
4 cloves garlic, minced
2 teaspoons oregano
2 cans (7 oz. each) **ORTEGA Green Chile Salsa**
Salt and pepper
2 tablespoons red wine vinegar
3 tablespoons oil

Combine all ingredients, except lamb. Pour over lamb cubes in a glass or enamel dish and mix thoroughly; cover and let stand overnight in refrigerator. Place lamb cubes on skewers and barbecue, basting with remaining marinade. *Serves 6*

69

Jamaican Fruit Lamb Chops

7 to 8 medium loin lamb chops
1 can (16 oz.) **DEL MONTE Lite Apricot Halves**
2 tsp. coffee crystals
Dash salt and pepper
2 Tbsp. chopped parsley

In large skillet, brown meat. Drain fruit reserving liquid in small saucepan. Heat liquid; stir in coffee to dissolve. Pour over meat; simmer 15 to 20 minutes, turning frequently. Add salt, pepper, fruit and parsley. Cover and heat through.   *3 to 4 servings*

Hearty Lamb Shanks

¼ cup all-purpose flour
1 teaspoon seasoned salt
½ teaspoon pepper
¼ teaspoon garlic powder
4 lamb shanks
2 tablespoons cooking oil
½ cup chopped onion
½ cup chopped carrot
¼ cup chopped celery
1 tablespoon chopped parsley
½ teaspoon rosemary
½ teaspoon salt
1 (1 lb.) can whole tomatoes
1 cup **LINDSAY® Pitted Ripe Olives**

Combine flour, seasoned salt, pepper and garlic powder. Coat shanks with flour mixture; reserve remaining flour. Heat oil in heavy skillet; brown shanks and remove from skillet. Add onion, carrot, celery, parsley, rosemary and salt to skillet and sauté lightly. Add tomatoes, ripe olives, and lamb shanks. Cover and simmer 2 to 2½ hours or until shanks are tender. Remove shanks to warm platter. Combine remaining flour mixture with a little cold water and add to pan. Cook, stirring until thickened. Pour over shanks.   *Makes 4 servings*

Barbecue

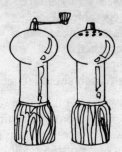

Summer Mixed Grill
Meat Kabobs

½ cup **WISH-BONE® Italian Dressing**
¼ cup dry white or red wine
1 teaspoon thyme
2 bay leaves
1½ pounds pork, chicken, lamb or beef cubes
Bacon slices (optional)

In large shallow baking dish, blend real Italian dressing, wine, thyme and bay leaves; add meat cubes. Cover and marinate in refrigerator, turning occasionally, 4 hours or overnight. Remove meat, reserving marinade. On skewers, alternately thread meat cubes and bacon. Grill or broil, turning and basting frequently with reserved marinade, until done.   *Makes about 6 servings*

Vegetable Kabobs

½ cup **WISH-BONE® Italian Dressing**
1 teaspoon finely chopped dill weed
3 cups assorted fresh vegetables

In large shallow baking dish, combine all ingredients. Cover and marinate in refrigerator, turning occasionally, 4 hours or overnight. Remove vegetables, reserving marinade. On skewers, alternately thread vegetables. During last 10 minutes of meat kabob cooking time, begin to grill or broil. Turn and baste frequently with reserved marinade until done.   *Makes about 6 servings*

Kikko Lamb Kabobs

½ cup wine vinegar
¼ cup **KIKKOMAN Soy Sauce**
2 tablespoons vegetable oil
2 teaspoons instant minced onion
1 clove garlic, crushed
¼ teaspoon pepper
1½ pounds fresh lamb shoulder, cut into 2-inch cubes

Combine vinegar, soy sauce, oil, onion, garlic and pepper in saucepan; bring to boil. Cool thoroughly; stir in lamb and marinate 2 to 3 hours. Arrange lamb on skewers; brush with marinade. Broil or grill to desired doneness, brushing with marinade.

Makes 4 servings

Beef and Vegetable Kabobs

½ cup olive or salad oil
2 tablespoons red wine vinegar
1 tablespoon **MORTON® NATURE'S SEASONS®**
Seasoning Blend
2 pounds boneless, tender beef, cubed for kabobs
½ pint cherry tomatoes
8 ounces fresh mushrooms, halved
4 medium onions, quartered
3 medium green peppers, cut into eighths
Pita or French bread rolls

Early in Day: In a large bowl, combine oil, vinegar, and seasoning blend; add beef cubes. Cover and refrigerate, stirring occasionally.

About 45 Minutes Before Serving: Prepare outdoor grill for barbecuing. Drain beef cubes, reserving marinade. On eight 18-inch skewers, alternately thread beef with vegetables. Heat reserved marinade to boiling; remove from heat. Brush beef and vegetables with marinade. Barbecue kabobs over medium coals 20 minutes for medium doneness, turning occasionally and brushing with marinade. Spoon into pita pockets or split rolls.

Makes 8 servings

OVEN BROILING METHOD:
Prepare kabobs as above. Place kabobs on rack in broiler pan. Broil 20 to 25 minutes to desired doneness, turning occasionally and brushing with marinade. Serve as above.

Central Park Kabobs

1½ pounds boneless chuck steak, cut into 1½" cubes
1½ teaspoons **ADOLPH'S® 100% Natural Meat Tenderizer-Seasoned**
1 can (8 oz.) tomato sauce
¼ cup brown sugar
2 tablespoons prepared mustard
1 teaspoon horseradish
1 medium green pepper, cut into 1" cubes
1 large onion, cut into wedges
6 cherry tomatoes
6 mushroom caps

Moisten meat with water. Sprinkle evenly on all sides with tenderizer and pierce deeply with a fork. (Use no salt.) In a saucepan, combine next four ingredients; heat through. Arrange meat on skewers, alternating with vegetables.

To barbecue: Grill kabobs 3" from heat about 15 minutes for medium, basting and turning frequently.

To cook indoors: Broil kabobs 4-5" from heat about 14 minutes for medium, basting and turning frequently.

Serves 6

Teriyaki Shish Kabobs

1 (3-pound) round steak (about 1½-inches thick), cut into cubes
1 (15¼-ounce) can pineapple chunks, drained
8 ounces (about 2 cups) small whole fresh mushrooms, cleaned
3 medium onions, quartered and separated into bite-size pieces
2 medium green peppers, cut into bite-size pieces
1 pint cherry tomatoes
Teriyaki Marinade*
Hot cooked rice

Prepare vegetables and meat; place all but tomatoes in large shallow baking dish. Pour Teriyaki Marinade on top. Marinate overnight; stir occasionally. Skewer marinated ingredients with tomatoes and pineapple chunks. Grill or broil to desired doneness; brush with marinade during cooking. Serve over rice. Refrigerate leftovers.   *Makes 8 servings*

*Teriyaki Marinade

1 cup firmly-packed **COLONIAL® Light Golden Brown Sugar**
⅔ cup catsup
⅔ cup vinegar
½ cup soy sauce
½ cup vegetable oil
5 to 6 cloves garlic, finely chopped
2 teaspoons ground ginger

In medium bowl, combine ingredients; mix well.

Tip: Teriyaki Marinade is also delicious when used to marinate pork chops or chicken.

Sierra Ranch Ribs

4 pounds country-style spareribs, trimmed and cut into
  serving pieces
Water
1 can (8 oz.) tomato sauce
1 cup chopped onion
½ cup **KARO® Dark Corn Syrup**
¼ cup cider vinegar
2 tablespoons Worcestershire sauce
1 teaspoon salt
1 teaspoon monosodium glutamate
1 teaspoon dry mustard
½ teaspoon chili powder

In 5-quart kettle place spareribs; add water to depth of 1″. Cover.
Bring to boil over high heat; reduce heat and boil gently 1 hour or
until ribs are fork tender. In 1-quart saucepan mix together remaining ingredients. Bring to boil; reduce heat; simmer 10 minutes.
Drain ribs. Brush generously with sauce.

To grill: Place ribs 6″ from source of heat, basting and turning
frequently, about 15 minutes or until browned.

To broil: Place ribs on broiler pan. Broil 4″ from source of heat,
basting occasionally, about 10 minutes on each side. If desired,
heat remaining sauce and serve with ribs.

Makes 6 to 8 servings

Barbecue Chicken,
Southern Style

1 cup **HEINZ Tomato Ketchup**
2-3 tablespoons honey
1 tablespoon lemon juice
Dash hot pepper sauce
2 to 2½ pounds broiler-fryer pieces
Salt and pepper

Combine ketchup, honey, lemon juice and hot pepper sauce.
Brush on chicken during last 5 to 10 minutes of grilling or broiling
time. Season with salt and pepper.

Makes 4-6 servings (about 1¼ cups sauce)

Sausages

Tuscany Sausage Skillet

8 sweet Italian sausages (about 1 lb.) sliced
⅓ cup water
1 package (10 oz.) **BIRDS EYE®** Italian Style
  Vegetables With a Seasoned Sauce

Brown sausages well in skillet. Add water and simmer 5 minutes. Move sausages to one side of skillet. Add vegetables. Bring to a *full* boil over medium heat, separate vegetables with a fork; stir frequently. Reduce heat; cover and simmer for 2 minutes.

Makes about 3½ cups or 3 servings

Sausage and Vegetables Alfresco

3 Tbsp. olive oil or butter
¼ cup chopped onions
¼ cup chopped green pepper
½ lb. fresh mushrooms, sliced
2 cups broccoli flowerettes, chopped asparagus, zucchini
  squash or green peas
1 Tbsp. chopped pimiento
¼ tsp. garlic powder
1 tsp. oregano
1 pound **HILLSHIRE FARM®** Smoked Sausage or
  Italian Smoked Sausage, cut into bite-sized pieces
¾ cup Parmesan cheese
Salt
Pepper
Cooked and buttered pasta

Stir-fry onions, green pepper, mushrooms, green vegetables, pimiento and seasonings in oil over medium high heat until crisp-tender (about 4 minutes). Add sausage and cook over medium heat until sausage is heated through, about 5 minutes, stirring often. Mix in ½ cup cheese, salt and pepper to taste. Serve over buttered pasta. Sprinkle with remaining ¼ cup cheese.

Yield: 4-6 servings

MICROWAVE METHOD:

Combine olive oil, onions and green pepper in a large glass bowl or casserole. Microwave, uncovered, HIGH, 3 minutes, stirring once. Add mushrooms, green vegetables, pimiento, garlic, oregano and sausage. Microwave, uncovered, HIGH, 3-5 minutes or until hot and crisp-tender, stirring once. Stir in ½ cup of cheese, salt and pepper to taste. Serve over buttered pasta. Sprinkle with remaining ¼ cup cheese.

Stir-Fry Pineapple Brown 'n Serve™

8 ounce package SWIFT PREMIUM® Original BROWN 'N SERVE™ Sausage Links
1 pound 4 ounce can pineapple chunks in juice, drained—reserve ¾ cup juice
1 cup sliced celery
1 green pepper cut into chunks
1 cup sliced fresh mushrooms
¼ cup water
1 tablespoon cornstarch
½ teaspoon ginger
¼ cup dry sherry
2 medium-size tomatoes cut into wedges
½ cup blanched almonds, optional

Cut sausage into halves lengthwise. Brown in skillet or electric wok. Add celery, green pepper and mushrooms. Stir-fry until vegetables are tender-crisp, about 5 to 6 minutes. Combine reserved pineapple juice, water, cornstarch, ginger and sherry. Mix well. Add to skillet, stirring constantly. Cook until liquid thickens. Stir in pineapple chunks and tomatoes. Cook an additional 2 to 3 minutes. Sprinkle with almonds, if desired.

Yield: 4 to 5 servings

German Sausage Skillet

6 slices bacon
1 medium (about 2 pounds) firm head green cabbage, cut into 6 wedges and cored
1 medium onion, chopped
2 Tbsp. sugar
¼ cup water
1 tsp. minced garlic
1 tsp. seasoned salt
½ tsp. crushed red pepper (optional)
2 tsp. caraway seed
1 lb. **HILLSHIRE FARM®** Polska Kielbasa, cut into 6 pieces

In a large skillet, fry bacon until crisp. Remove. Add the following ingredients to the drippings: cabbage, onion, sugar, water and spices. Cook, covered, over medium heat, 10-15 minutes, stirring several times. Add **Polska Kielbasa**. Return cover and continue to cook 10-15 minutes or until the sausage is heated. Top with reserved bacon, crumbled.   *Yield: 6 servings*

MICROWAVE METHOD:
Place bacon in a 2 qt. glass baking dish. Microwave, covered with a paper towel, HIGH, 5-6 minutes or until crisp. Remove bacon and drain. Stir the following ingredients into the drippings: onion, sugar, water, and spices. Add cabbage wedges. Microwave, covered, HIGH, 8 minutes. Move cabbage wedges to the side of the dish. Place sausage in the center. Microwave, covered, HIGH, 5-10 minutes or until sausage is hot and cabbage is tender. Top with reserved bacon, crumbled.

German Brand Wieners 'n Kraut

1 lb. pkg. **JOHN MORRELL®** German Brand Wieners
2 cans (14 oz. each) sauerkraut, drained
3 cups of beer
1 large onion, thinly sliced
½ cup thinly sliced celery

Place kraut and beer in a large saucepan and bring to a boil; reduce heat and simmer, covered, for 20 minutes. Add **German Brand Wieners**, onion and celery. Bring to a boil, reduce heat and then simmer another 20 minutes. To serve, place kraut mixture on heated serving dish and top with **German Brand Wieners**.

Yield: 6 servings

Sausages Español

1 package (16 oz.) **JONES Dinner Sausages**
½ cup onion, coarsely chopped
½ cup celery, coarsely chopped
¾ cup green pepper, coarsely chopped
1 can (16 oz.) tomatoes, coarsely chopped, with juice
1 can (8 oz.) tomato sauce
2 cloves garlic, finely chopped
½ tsp. dried thyme
Salt, pepper, and a dash of hot pepper sauce to taste

Prepare **JONES Dinner Sausages** according to directions, remove from pan and keep warm. Pour off all but 2 tablespoons of fat, add onions, celery and green pepper, sauté for 5 minutes. Add tomatoes with juice, tomato sauce, garlic, thyme. Simmer, uncovered, for 15 minutes. Season to taste, return sausages to pan long enough to reheat. Serve with rice or pasta, accompanied by green salad.

Smokie Spanish Rice

1 package (12 oz.) **OSCAR MAYER Smokie Links** sausages
1 cup uncooked long grain rice
1 can (1 lb.) ready-seasoned stewed tomatoes
1 can (8 oz.) tomato sauce
½ cup water
1 bay leaf
½ teaspoon salt
½ teaspoon ground thyme

Cut **Smokie Links** into bite-sized pieces. Combine in a large skillet with remaining ingredients. Cover and bring to a boil. Simmer 30 minutes, stirring occasionally.

Makes 4-6 servings

All-American Sausage Stew

1 can (10½ ounces) condensed beef broth
1 cup water
⅛ teaspoon pepper
1 bay leaf
2 medium onions, quartered
6 carrots, pared, cut in julienne pieces
1½ cups diced celery
2 potatoes, pared, diced
2 tablespoons water
1 tablespoon all-purpose flour
1 pound **ECKRICH® Smoked Sausage**, cut in ½" pieces
Salt to taste
Grated Parmesan cheese

Combine broth, 1 cup water, pepper, bay leaf, and vegetables except potatoes in a 4-quart saucepot. Simmer, covered, 10 minutes. Add potatoes; cook until vegetables are tender. Remove bay leaf. Mix 2 tablespoons water with flour; stir into vegetables. Add sausage; heat. Add salt. Top each serving with cheese.

6 to 8 servings

MICROWAVE METHOD:
Combine broth, 1 cup water, pepper, bay leaf, and vegetables except potatoes in a 3-quart glass baking dish. Cook, covered, 14 minutes, stirring twice. Add potatoes; cook 12 minutes, stirring twice. Remove bay leaf. Mix 2 tablespoons water with flour; stir into vegetables. Add sausage; cook, uncovered, 6 minutes, stirring once. Add salt. Let stand 5 minutes before serving.

Poultry

Holiday Stuffed Roaster

½ cup chopped celery
¼ cup sliced green onion
7 tablespoons butter or margarine
2 cups coarse dry bread crumbs
1 cup chopped drained raw oysters
¼ cup oyster liquid
2 tablespoons chopped fresh parsley
½ teaspoon salt
½ teaspoon poultry seasoning
⅛ teaspoon pepper
1 **PERDUE® Oven Stuffer Roaster**

Sauté celery and onion in 6 tablespoons butter until tender. Remove from heat. Blend in bread, oysters, oyster liquid, parsley and spices. Pre-heat oven to 350°F. Stuff bird with oyster mixture. Tie legs together. Dot with remaining 1 tablespoon butter. Season with salt and pepper.

Roast 2¼ to 2¾ hours for 5-6 pound bird; 2½ to 3 hours for 6 to 7 pound bird.

Wessonality Fried Chicken

Combine ¾ cup flour, 1½ tsp. salt, ¾ tsp. paprika and ¼ tsp. pepper in a bag. Shake 3 lbs. chicken pieces, a few at a time, in bag. Dip chicken in 1 egg beaten with 2 Tbsp. water. Shake in flour mixture again. Fry in 12-inch skillet in 3 cups **WESSON® Oil** heated to 375° 20 to 30 minutes, turning once.   *Makes 6 servings*

Chicken With Tangy Lemon Gravy

1 cup sliced onion
1 cup thinly sliced carrots
1 cup thinly sliced celery
1 lemon, sliced
1 clove garlic, minced
1½ teaspoons salt
½ teaspoon dried thyme leaves
¼ teaspoon pepper
3 whole broiler-fryer chicken breasts, halved
¼ cup **MAZOLA®/NUCOA® Margarine**, melted
1 pound zucchini, thinly sliced
2 tablespoons **ARGO®/KINGSFORD'S® Corn Starch**
1½ cups cool chicken bouillon or water

In shallow roasting pan mix together onion, carrots, celery, lemon, garlic, salt, thyme and pepper. Place chicken, skin side up, on top. Pour melted margarine over chicken. Bake in 375°F oven 30 minutes. Add zucchini, bake 30 minutes longer or until vegetables are tender. Remove chicken, zucchini and lemon to serving platter. Mix corn starch and bouillon until smooth; pour into pan. Stirring constantly, bring to boil over medium heat and boil 1 minute. Serve with chicken and vegetables.

Makes 4 to 6 servings

Note: 1 broiler-fryer chicken, cut up, may be substituted for chicken breasts.
Makes 4 servings

Versatile Chicken

1 (3-pound) broiler-fryer chicken, cut up
¾ cup buttermilk
1 tablespoon **WYLER'S® Chicken-Flavor Instant Bouillon**
½ teaspoon oregano leaves, optional
1 cup unsifted flour
1 to 2 teaspoons paprika
¼ cup melted margarine or butter

Rinse chicken; pat dry with paper towels. In a 1-cup measure, combine buttermilk, bouillon and oregano. Mix well. Let stand 10 minutes; stir. Place chicken in large bowl. Pour bouillon mixture over chicken; toss to coat. Let stand at least 30 minutes to blend flavors. In paper or plastic bag, combine flour and paprika. Add chicken, a few pieces at a time; shake to coat. Place in 13x9-inch baking dish. Drizzle with margarine. Bake uncovered in preheated 350° oven for 1 hour or until golden. Refrigerate leftovers.

Makes 4 servings

Tip: To fry chicken, omit melted margarine; fry in vegetable oil.

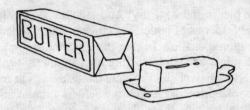

Home Style Chicken in Mustard Sauce

5 packets **G. WASHINGTON'S® Golden Seasoning and Broth Mix**
½ cup flour
1 chicken, cut in pieces
¼ cup butter or margarine
1 cup water
1 tablespoon chopped scallions
1 teaspoon tarragon
3 tablespoons **GULDEN'S® Spicy Brown Mustard**
1 cup half and half

Combine 3 packets of seasoning and broth with flour; coat chicken pieces. Brown chicken pieces in butter until golden. Dissolve remaining 2 packets of seasoning and broth in 1 cup water. Add to skillet along with scallions and tarragon. Cover; continue cooking over low heat until sauce begins to thicken and chicken is fork tender. Mix mustard with half and half. Pour over simmered chicken; stir gently; cover. Allow to simmer 10 more minutes.

Serves 4

Baked Yogurt Chicken

1 cut up frying chicken, 2½ to 3 pounds
Salt, pepper
6 Tbsp. butter or margarine
2 Tbsp. flour
1 Tbsp. paprika
2 cups **DANNON® Plain Yogurt**
¼ pound fresh mushrooms, cleaned and sliced
2 Tbsp. fresh lemon juice
2 Tbsp. chopped fresh dill or parsley

Wash chicken pieces and wipe dry. Add salt and pepper. In a large pan, melt 4 tablespoons of butter, fry chicken until golden brown. Remove to buttered shallow baking dish. Sprinkle flour and paprika into pan juices and cook, stirring for 1 minute. Stir in yogurt and mix well. Spoon over chicken. Sauté mushrooms in remaining 2 tablespoons of butter and lemon juice for 1 minute and spoon over pan. Sprinkle with the dill. Bake, covered, in preheated moderate oven (325°F.) for about 1¼ hours, or until chicken is tender. *Serves about 4*

Honey 'n' Spice Barbecue Chicken

½ cup **HEINZ 57 Sauce**
¼ cup honey
2 to 2½ pounds broiler-fryer pieces
Melted butter or margarine

Combine **57 Sauce** and honey. Place the chicken pieces on broiler pan or grill; brush with melted butter, then **57 Sauce**-honey mixture. Broil or grill until chicken is tender, turning and basting frequently with honey mixture. *Makes 4-5 servings*

Note: For a flavorful sauce to serve over slices of ham or meat loaf, combine 2 parts **HEINZ 57 Sauce** and 1 part honey.

Italian Chicken

3½ pounds chicken pieces
Salt and pepper
¼ cup **BERTOLLI® Olive Oil**
1 medium onion, thinly sliced
8 ounces mushrooms, sliced
2 cloves garlic, minced
1 teaspoon dried basil leaves
½ teaspoon dried oregano leaves
¼ teaspoon salt
2 cups **BERTOLLI® Spaghetti Sauce**
½ cup sliced ripe olives
½ cup **BERTOLLI® Soave Wine**
1 jar (6 ounces) marinated artichoke hearts, drained

Sprinkle chicken with salt and pepper; sauté in oil in Dutch oven until brown; remove. Sauté onion, mushrooms, garlic, basil, oregano and ¼ teaspoon salt 3 minutes. Stir in sauce, olives and wine. Add chicken, spooning sauce over. Heat to boiling. Reduce heat; simmer covered until chicken is tender, about 45 minutes. Stir in artichokes; cook 3 minutes.   *Makes 6 servings*

Stage Coach Chicken

⅔ cup prepared **HIDDEN VALLEY ORIGINAL RANCH® Salad Dressing**
1 egg, slightly beaten
1 2½ to 3-pound broiler-fryer, cut-up
⅓ cup all purpose flour
1 teaspoon salt
¼ teaspoon pepper
1 cup cornflake crumbs
¼ cup butter or margarine, melted

In a bowl, combine Salad Dressing and egg; set aside. Rinse chicken with water and drain well. Dredge chicken pieces in flour mixed with salt and pepper; dip in Salad Dressing-egg mixture; roll in cornflake crumbs. Arrange chicken pieces in a broiler pan, lined with foil if desired. Drizzle with butter. Bake at 350°F. for 50 minutes to 1 hour or until fork tender.

Makes 4 to 6 servings

Tandoori Chicken
(Low Calorie/Low Fat)

1 2½- to 3-pound broiler-fryer, cut up
1 teaspoon cayenne
1 teaspoon paprika
¼ cup lemon juice
6 tablespoons red wine vinegar
¾ cup chopped onions
¼ cup chopped pimiento
¾ cup plain low-fat yogurt
1 packet **BUTTER BUDS**®, mixed with ¼ cup hot water
¼ teaspoon ginger

Preheat oven to 375°F. Wash, dry, and skin chicken. Prick in several places with sharp knife point. Arrange chicken in glass baking dish. In separate bowl, mix cayenne and paprika with lemon juice and vinegar. Rub into chicken. Refrigerate 1 hour. In blender container, combine onions, pimiento, yogurt, **BUTTER BUDS**®, and ginger. Cover and process at medium speed 10 seconds. Pour yogurt mixture over chicken. Bake 40 to 50 minutes, or until tender. Baste frequently with yogurt mixture while cooking.   *4 servings*

Per Serving (¼ chicken): Calories: 245; Fat: 6g

Note: By using **BUTTER BUDS**® instead of butter in this recipe, you have saved 188 calories and 70 mg cholesterol per serving.

Crunchy Baked Chicken Variations

Wash 3 lbs. frying chicken pieces. Pat dry. For any of the following variations, dip chicken in liquid mixture. Coat evenly with **KELLOGG'S**® **CORN FLAKE CRUMBS** mixture. Place in single layer, skin side up, in well-greased or foil-lined shallow baking pan. Drizzle with 3 tablespoons melted margarine or butter, if desired. Bake at 350°F. about 1 hour or until chicken is tender. Do not cover pan or turn chicken while baking.

Yield: 6 servings

VARIATIONS:

Corn-Crisped Chicken

Dip in ½ cup evaporated milk. Coat with mixture of 1 cup **KELLOGG'S® CORN FLAKE CRUMBS**, 1 teaspoon salt and ⅛ teaspoon pepper.

California Crusty Chicken

Dip in mixture of ¼ cup melted margarine or butter, 3 tablespoons lemon juice and 1 teaspoon grated lemon peel. Coat with mixture of 1¼ cups **KELLOGG'S® CORN FLAKE CRUMBS**, 1 teaspoon salt and ¼ teaspoon pepper.

Baked Chicken Italiano

Dip in ½ cup Italian-style salad dressing. Coat with 1¼ cups **KELLOGG'S® CORN FLAKE CRUMBS**. If desired, marinate chicken in dressing for at least 1 hour.

® Kellogg Company

Easy Chicken Cacciatore

- 1 clove garlic, minced
- 1 medium green pepper, sliced into ¼" strips
- 2 tablespoons vegetable oil
- 1 chicken (2½-3 pounds), cut up
- 1 jar (15½ oz.) **RAGU®️ Spaghetti Sauce**
- ½ package (16 oz. size) seashell pasta, cooked and drained

Preheat oven to 350°F. In a large skillet, sauté garlic and pepper in oil until tender; remove and set aside. Brown chicken on both sides; cook 30 minutes or until tender. Add spaghetti sauce and green peppers; simmer, covered, 10 minutes. Place pasta in an 11" × 7" baking dish; spoon chicken and sauce over pasta. Bake, covered, 20 minutes or until bubbly.   *Serves 4*

Ranch Chicken

1 3-pound (4 cups) chicken
1 medium onion, peeled and left whole
1 rib celery
2 teaspoons salt
1 10½-ounce can cream of chicken soup
⅔ cup tomatoes with chilies
4 cups **FRITOS® Brand Corn Chips**
2 cups grated American cheese
1 cup chopped onion
2 tablespoons shortening

In kettle cook chicken until tender with onion, celery, salt and enough water to cover. Bone chicken and cube. Strain broth, reserving 1⅓ cups.

Sauté chopped onion in shortening. Add soup, tomatoes, and broth. Simmer 5 minutes.

In electric skillet, spread a layer of chicken, **FRITOS® Brand Corn Chips**, sauce and cheese. Repeat, ending with cheese. Cover and cook at 250° F. for 20 minutes. Lower temperature to 200° F. and continue cooking for 40 minutes.

Makes 6 to 8 servings

Arroz con Pollo

2½ pounds cut-up chicken
1 envelope **SHAKE 'N BAKE® Seasoned Coating Mix for Chicken—Barbecue Style**
2 tablespoons butter or margarine
1½ cups **MINUTE® Rice**
½ cup chopped onion
1 small clove garlic, crushed (optional)
1½ cups water
1 package (10 oz.) **BIRDS EYE® 5 Minute Sweet Green Peas**, thawed
1 can (4 oz.) sliced mushrooms, drained
chicken bouillon cubes
nch of ground bay leaves (optional)

ken with seasoned coating mix as directed on package.
3 × 9-inch pan. Sprinkle evenly with any remaining

mix. Bake at 350° for 50 minutes, or until chicken is tender. Meanwhile, melt butter in skillet or saucepan. Add rice, onion and garlic and sauté until rice is lightly browned. Add remaining ingredients. Bring to a boil. Remove from heat; cover and let stand 5 minutes. Serve with the chicken.

Makes 5 cups rice mixture plus chicken or 4 servings

Tropical Chicken
(Low Calorie/Low Fat)

2½ lbs. quartered chicken parts
8 oz. can crushed pineapple packed in unsweetened juice
½ cup **ESTEE® Granulated Fructose**
2 Tbsp. lemon juice
1 tsp. dry mustard powder

Preheat oven to 375°F. Remove excess fat from beneath skin and cut chicken into parts. Rinse each piece in cold water and pat dry. Mix pineapple with its juice, fructose, lemon juice and mustard together in small bowl. Place chicken on rack in shallow baking pan. Spread pineapple mixture over each piece of chicken, approx. 2 tablespoons each. Bake for 20 minutes, then remove from oven to baste again. Bake 20 minutes and baste again. Return to oven for final 20 minutes of baking. Pour pineapple sauce and drippings from baking pan into bowl and chill. Skim fat, then return to sauce pan to reheat. Serve sauce over chicken.   *Makes 6 servings*

NUTRITION INFORMATION

Calories	Carbohydrates	Protein	Fat	Cholesterol	Sodium
185	22g	28g	3g	55mg	64 mg

DIABETIC EXCHANGE INFORMATION

Fruit	Meat
2	4 (med. fat)

Florentine Chicken

3 whole chicken breasts, split (about 3 lb.)
¼ teaspoon salt
Dash of paprika
2 tablespoons butter or margarine
1 package (10 oz.) **BIRDS EYE® 5 Minute Chopped Spinach**
1½ cups very hot water
¼ cup softened butter or margarine
1 package (6 oz.) **STOVE TOP® Chicken Flavor Stuffing Mix**
1 tablespoon lemon juice
½ cup sour cream

Place chicken, skin side up, in 3-quart shallow baking dish. Sprinkle with salt and paprika; dot with 2 tablespoons butter. Bake at 400° for 30 minutes. Meanwhile, prepare spinach as directed on package; drain well, squeezing out all liquid. Combine hot water, ¼ cup butter and contents of Vegetable/Seasoning Packet in a bowl, stirring until butter is melted. Add Stuffing Crumbs, lemon juice, sour cream and the spinach; stir just to moisten. Move chicken to one side of dish; baste with pan drippings. Mound stuffing on other side and bake 15 minutes longer.

Makes 4 cups stuffing plus chicken or 6 servings

Pineapple Chicken Oriental

½ cup **WISH-BONE® Italian Dressing**
1 can (20 oz.) crushed pineapple, drained (reserve liquid)
3 tablespoons firmly packed brown sugar
½ teaspoon ground ginger
4 whole chicken breasts skinned, boned, and pounded
⅓ cup finely chopped green pepper
⅓ cup slivered almonds
1 tablespoon cornstarch

In shallow baking dish, combine Italian dressing, reserved liquid, sugar, and ginger; mix well. Add chicken and marinate 3 hours in refrigerator, turning occasionally.

Preheat oven to 375°. In small bowl, combine pineapple, green pepper, and almonds. Remove chicken; drain and reserve marinade. Spread ¼ pineapple mixture on each chicken breast; roll up and place seam side down in baking dish. Pour ¼ cup marinade over chicken and bake 35 minutes or until chicken is tender.

Remove chicken to heated platter. In small saucepan, combine cooked and reserved marinades with cornstarch; heat, stirring constantly, until slightly thickened, about 2 minutes. Serve over chicken. *Makes 4 servings*

Chicken Maryland

3 pounds frying chicken pieces
½ cup KIKKOMAN Teriyaki Sauce
2 eggs
6 tablespoons water, divided
½ cup flour
1½ cups dry bread crumbs
Vegetable oil for frying

Gravy:
2 tablespoons flour
1 cup milk
1 cup water
1 tablespoon KIKKOMAN Soy Sauce

Place chicken and teriyaki sauce in large plastic bag; press air out and close top securely. Refrigerate 8 hours or overnight; turn bag over occasionally. Beat eggs together with 2 tablespoons water. Remove chicken from marinade; coat with ½ cup flour. Dip into egg mixture; then roll in bread crumbs. Pour enough oil in large frying pan or electric frying pan to measure ¼ inch; heat to 350°F. Brown chicken pieces on all sides in hot oil over medium heat. Remove chicken; pour off and discard oil. Return chicken to pan; pour in remaining 4 tablespoons water. Cover and simmer 20 minutes, or until chicken is tender. Remove chicken; keep warm while preparing gravy. Blend together flour and milk; stir into pan drippings with water and soy sauce. Cook until mixture boils and thickens, stirring constantly. Serve gravy with chicken.

Makes 4 to 6 servings

Cheesy Cookin' Good™ Chicken Rolls

2 large **COOKIN' GOOD**™ **Chicken Breasts**, boned,
   halved and skin removed
2 slices of Swiss cheese
1 tablespoon spicy mustard
½ cup seasoned bread crumbs
Melted butter or margarine approx. ½ cup
Paprika
Parsley

Arrange sliced Swiss cheese over chicken breasts. Trim if necessary. Lightly spread mustard over cheese and roll starting at
narrow end. Secure with toothpicks. Dip first into melted butter or
margarine then into bread crumbs. Sprinkle with paprika and
parsley. Place rolls on a baking dish. Microwave for 6-8 minutes
or 15 minutes in toaster oven or conventional oven at 350°F. Serve
with herbed rice and a crisp salad.   *Serves 4*

Honey-Gold Chicken

4 chicken breasts, quartered
1 cup **GOLDEN DIPT®** **Chicken Seasoned Coating**
   Mix
1 tsp. salt
½ tsp. pepper
1 6-oz. can frozen lemonade concentrate
¼ lb. butter
½ cup honey
1 lemon, cut in wedges
Parsley sprigs

Dip chicken breasts in mixture of dry ingredients. Melt butter in
shallow pan in 400° oven. Place chicken in pan, coating it with
butter. Bake 30 minutes; turn. Combine lemonade concentrate
with honey. Pour over chicken; bake 45 minutes at 325°, turning
and basting every 15 minutes. When chicken is fork-tender, trans-
fer to warm platter, garnish with lemon wedges and parsley.
                                                       Serves 4

East-West Chicken Drumsticks

(Microwave Recipe)

2 pounds **COUNTRY PRIDE**® **Broiler-Fryer Chicken Drumsticks**
1 cup corn flake crumbs
1 teaspoon salt
⅛ teaspoon pepper
½ cup evaporated milk
1 tablespoon soy sauce
Mustard Sauce*

Mix corn flake crumbs with salt and pepper in shallow dish. Mix evaporated milk and soy sauce in another shallow dish. Dip chicken drumsticks in evaporated milk, then roll immediately in seasoned corn flake crumbs. Place drumsticks in lightly greased 12 × 7½ × 2-inch glass baking dish. Cover with waxed paper and cook in microwave oven 10 minutes, turn dish, cook 8 to 10 minutes longer. Let stand 3 to 5 minutes. Serve with Mustard Sauce if desired. Total cooking time: 20 minutes.

Yield: 4 to 6 servings

*Mustard Sauce

¼ cup prepared mustard
1 teaspoon sugar
½ teaspoon salt
⅛ teaspoon **TABASCO**® **Pepper Sauce**
½ cup evaporated milk
1 teaspoon lemon juice

In small glass bowl or 2-cup glass measuring cup mix all ingredients except lemon juice. Cover with waxed paper and cook in microwave oven 2 minutes. Stir in lemon juice. Serve with chicken drumsticks. Cooking time: 2 minutes.   *Yield: ¼ cup*

Note: 2 pounds **COUNTRY PRIDE**® **Chicken Wings** may be substituted for drumsticks.

Breast of Chicken
en Croûte

2 chicken breasts, boned, skinned and cut in half
Salt, pepper, oregano
1 package (10 ounces) frozen chopped spinach, thawed
    and squeezed dry
1 teaspoon minced garlic
3 tablespoons processed cheese spread
1 package (17¼ ounces) **PEPPERIDGE FARM®**
    "Frozen Bake It" Fresh Puff Pastry
4 slices ham
1 egg beaten with 1 teaspoon water
½ pint sour cream

Sprinkle chicken breasts lightly with salt, pepper and oregano.
Combine spinach, garlic and cheese spread and season to taste
with salt and pepper. Thaw pastry sheets 20 minutes, then unfold.
Cut each sheet into 4 squares. On a lightly floured surface, roll
first square until it's slightly larger than the chicken breast. In
center of pastry place a slice of ham folded in half, ¼ of the
spinach mixture and a chicken breast. Roll second square of pastry
only enough to cover chicken breast and border of the first sheet.
Press edges together firmly to seal and trim with pastry wheel. If
desired, use scraps to decorate pastry and attach with beaten egg.
Repeat with remaining chicken and pastry. Place on baking sheet;
brush top with egg and bake in preheated 375° oven for 30 minutes
or until golden brown. Serve with sour cream.

Makes 4 servings

Glazed Drumsticks

1 pkg. **HOLLY FARMS® Drumsticks**
1 tsp. salt
¼ cup honey
1 Tbsp. soy sauce
1 Tbsp. all-purpose flour
½ cup cold water

Preheat oven to 350°F. Place drumsticks in shallow baking dish. Bake for 45 minutes. Combine salt, soy sauce, honey and baste chicken. Cover chicken and baste occasionally while cooking for an additional 15 minutes or until tender. Remove chicken to serving dish, pour pan juices in small skillet. Blend ½ cup cold water into flour, stir into pan juices. Cook, stirring constantly, until thickened and bubbly. Serve sauce with drumsticks.

Golden Gate Chicken, Cantonese

⅓ cup **SUN-MAID® Golden Seedless Raisins**
1 (13¾ oz.) can chicken broth
1 tablespoon chopped fresh ginger (or ¾ teaspoon powdered ginger)
2½ teaspoons soy sauce
2 tablespoons cornstarch
¼ cup dry sherry
2 teaspoons sugar
3 tablespoons vinegar
2 lbs. boned, skinned chicken breasts
Batter*
½ cup cooking oil

Bring first 4 ingredients to simmer. Blend cornstarch, sherry and sugar; stir into sauce and cook clear. Add vinegar; keep warm. Cut chicken in 1½ inch chunks. Dip in Batter, drain and fry until golden in heated oil. Cook single layer at a time. Combine with hot sauce. *Makes 6 servings*

*Batter

Beat together ½ cup each sifted flour and water, 1 egg, 1 teaspoon onion powder, ¾ teaspoon salt.

Chinese Imperial Chicken

1¼ lbs. skinned, boned chicken breasts, cut into 1-inch pieces

Marinade:
2 tablespoons LA CHOY® Soy Sauce
1½ teaspoons dry vermouth
1 teaspoon Oriental sesame oil
2 tablespoons cold water
1 tablespoon cornstarch

Spinach mixture:
2 packages (10 oz. each) frozen spinach
1 teaspoon salt
1 teaspoon Oriental sesame oil
1 tablespoon minced garlic

Vegetable mixture:
2 tablespoons chopped green onion
2 tablespoons minced fresh ginger
2 tablespoons minced garlic
3 cans (8 oz. each) LA CHOY® Water Chestnuts, drained and halved

Sauce mixture:
2 tablespoons dry vermouth
3 tablespoons LA CHOY® Soy Sauce
1½ tablespoons sugar
1½ teaspoons Oriental sesame oil
2½ teaspoons Worcestershire sauce
½ teaspoon hot pepper sauce, or to taste
⅓ cup chicken broth
1 tablespoon cornstarch

Cooking oil
1½ cups roasted cashews (if salted, shake in sieve to remove salt)

Combine all ingredients for marinade and pour over chicken, mixing well. Let stand 20 minutes at room temperature.

Meanwhile, cook spinach according to package directions. Rinse under cold water to stop cooking; drain. Toss with seasonings. Arrange around border of serving platter. Set aside.

Combine vegetable mixture; set aside. Combine sauce mixture; set aside.

In wok or deep saucepan, heat oil for deep frying. Drain chicken pieces; fry a few at a time until golden brown. Drain on paper towels.

In a large skillet or wok placed over medium high heat, heat three tablespoons cooking oil. Add vegetable mixture; cook and stir 1 minute. Add sauce mixture; cook and stir until sauce thickens. Add chicken pieces and cashews; cook and stir 1 or 2 minutes or until chicken is heated through. Spoon into center of service platter. Serve immediately.   *4 servings*

Spanish Chicken Stew

1 5-lb. stewing chicken, whole or cut up
3 tablespoons POMPEIAN Olive Oil
1 tablespoon salt
12 small whole new potatoes, peeled
2 carrots, diced
1½ cups water
1 package frozen peas
1 package frozen artichoke hearts
2 tablespoons flour

Place chicken in **POMPEIAN Olive Oil** in large, heavy pot. Add salt, cover, turn heat low as possible and steam chicken in **POMPEIAN** for 1 hour. (Chicken should not brown.) Add potatoes, carrots and water; cover, continue cooking over lowest heat 1 hour longer or until chicken is very tender, adding water if necessary. Add frozen peas and artichokes, cook until frozen blocks can be broken up, cook 5 minutes longer. Skim fat from top of sauce. Mix flour with liquid from pot to make thin paste, add this to sauce, and cook until sauce is smooth and thickened. Serve vegetables with chicken on large platter. *Makes 12 servings*

Flaky Crescent Chicken Wellington

10-oz. pkg. frozen chopped spinach, cooked and well
    drained
2 cups chopped cooked chicken or 2 (5-oz.) cans boned
    chicken, drained and flaked
3 hard-cooked eggs, chopped
½ cup finely chopped dill pickle (reserve 2 tablespoons
    liquid for sauce)
⅓ cup finely chopped celery
2 (8-oz.) cans **PILLSBURY Refrigerated Quick
Crescent Dinner Rolls***
¼ cup **PARKAY Margarine** or butter, melted
½ teaspoon dry mustard

Sauce:
1 cup dairy sour cream
2 tablespoons reserved dill pickle liquid

Heat oven to 350°F. Grease cookie sheet. In large bowl, combine
spinach, chicken, eggs, dill pickle and celery. Set aside. Unroll 1
can of dough into 2 long rectangles. Overlap long sides ½ inch;
firmly pressing edges and perforations to seal. Press or roll to form
12x9-inch rectangle. Combine margarine and mustard; brush half
over dough. Spread half the chicken mixture over seasoned margarine to within 1 inch of edges. Starting at seam-side-down on
one side of prepared cookie sheet. Repeat with second can of
dough and remaining filling. Cut 2-inch diagonal slashes at 2-inch
intervals across tops of Wellingtons. Bake at 350°F. for 18 to 28
minutes or until deep golden brown. Cool slightly. Remove from
pan; place on serving plate. In small bowl, combine sauce ingredients. Slice to serve; serve with sauce. *8 to 10 servings*

*Tips: For best results, keep dough refrigerated until ready to use.
To reheat, cover loosely with foil; heat at 350°F. for 15 to 20
minutes.

NUTRITION INFORMATION PER SERVING

SERVING SIZE: 1/10 of recipe		Percent U.S. RDA	
Calories	320	Per Serving	
Protein	15 g	Protein	25%
Carbohydrate	22 g	Vitamin A	45%
Fat	19 g	Vitamin C	8%
Sodium	830 mg	Thiamine	10%
Potassium	290 mg	Riboflavin	10%
		Niacin	20%
		Calcium	6%
		Iron	10%

Chicken Pot Pie

4 cups chicken stock
1 cup diced carrots
1 cup peas, fresh or frozen
½ cup chopped celery
½ cup chopped onion
½ teaspoon salt
½ teaspoon black pepper
4 cups cooked diced chicken (or turkey)
¼ cup white flour
½ cup cold water
1 recipe, Pastry for Chicken Pot Pie*
Melted margarine

1.   Pour the chicken stock in a large pot. Add the carrots, peas, celery and onion and bring to a boil. Boil for 10 minutes. Add the salt, pepper and cooked chicken and continue to cook until the chicken is heated through.

2.   Combine the flour and water and form a paste. Slowly add to the chicken mixture, stirring constantly until slightly thickened.

3.   Line a 3-quart casserole with pastry and pour the filling into the casserole. Place the top layer of pastry over the filling and seal the edges as you would a pie. (Or place the filling into twelve individual ramekins 4½" in diameter and place pastry circles over the top of each.) Cut several small slashes in the top of the crust and brush with melted margarine.

4.   Bake in 375° oven for 45 minutes.   *Makes 12 servings*

*Pastry For Chicken Pot Pie

1 cup warm low-fat milk
1 package active dry yeast (check the date on the
package)
2 eggs lightly beaten
1 package **BATTER-LITE® Natural Sourdough Bread
Mix**
5 cups unbleached white flour
1 teaspoon salt
2 tablespoons **SWEETLITE™ Fructose**
½ cup unmelted corn oil margarine

1.   Pour the warm milk into a large warm mixing bowl and
sprinkle the yeast over the top of it. Stir until the yeast is dissolved, about 5 minutes.
2.   Add the lightly beaten eggs and **BATTER-LITE® Natural
Sourdough Bread Mix** and mix well.
3.   Combine 4 cups of the flour with the salt and fructose in a
warm bowl. Using a pastry blender (or 2 knives), cut the margarine into the flour mixture until it looks like coarse corn meal.
4.   Form a well in the center of the flour mixture and pour the
sourdough mixture into it. Mix well.
5.   Turn onto a floured board and knead the dough, adding the
remaining flour mixture until the dough is no longer sticky and is
easy to handle.
6.   Roll ¾ of the dough to form the lining of a 3-quart casserole
dish and ¼ of the dough to form the top crust (or make 12 4½"
circles to cover individual pot pies).

*Makes 12 individual 4½" circles or
a top and bottom crust for a casserole*

Zippy Cookin' Good™ Livers

4 slices of bacon
1 pound of **COOKIN' GOOD**™ Livers
1 medium onion, sliced

Sauce:

½ cup ketchup
2 tablespoons of brown sugar
1 tablespoon Worcestershire sauce
1 tablespoon lemon or lime juice
1 tablespoon prepared mustard
1 clove of crushed garlic or ¼ teaspoon of garlic powder
¼ teaspoon pepper

In an electric skillet or large frying pan, cook bacon until crisp; remove to drain on absorbent paper. In bacon fat sauté onion until tender; add livers and sauté until livers are no longer pink. While livers are cooking prepare sauce in a small mixing bowl by combining remaining ingredients, stirring to blend well. Pour sauce over livers and simmer until hot and bubbly. Serve with bacon crumbled over the top.   *Serves 2-3*

Polynesian Game Hens

6 **TYSON**® **Cornish Game Hens**
1½ cups honey
1½ cups prepared mustard
⅓ cup lemon juice
1 Tbsp. curry powder
Paprika
Rice or Chinese noodles
Fresh pineapple, garnish

Rinse hens, pat dry, and season with salt and pepper inside and out. Place in shallow baking pan. Baste hens with sweet and sour sauce (honey, mustard, lemon juice and curry powder). Bake 45-60 minutes in preheated oven at 400°F. Last 10 minutes, spoon mixture oven hens again and sprinkle with paprika. Serve with rice or Chinese noodles. Garnish with fresh pineapple.   *Serves 6*

Mole con Arroz

2 tablespoons vegetable oil
1 cup **BLUE RIBBON® Slivered Almonds**
1 cup chopped onion
1 medium clove garlic, minced
⅛ teaspoon cinnamon
⅛ teaspoon cloves
¼ teaspoon pepper
1 oz. unsweetened chocolate, coarsely chopped
2 cans (7 oz. each) green chile salsa
1 can (about 1 lb.) tomato sauce
2 cups bite-size pieces cooked turkey or chicken
4 portions hot cooked rice
1 avocado, sliced
1 orange, sliced
Dairy sour cream
BLUE RIBBON® Slivered Almonds (additional)

Heat oil in skillet, then sauté almonds, onion and garlic 10 minutes over medium heat, stirring often. Stir in next six ingredients; heat, stirring, until chocolate melts. Purée mixture in blender.

Return to skillet, stir in turkey; simmer about 5 minutes. Serve over rice and garnish with avocado, orange, dollops of sour cream and slivered almonds. *Makes 4 generous servings*

Turkey and Rice Medley

¼ cup diagonally sliced celery
¼ cup green pepper strips
1 small clove garlic, minced
¼ teaspoon ground ginger
2 tablespoons butter or margarine
1 can (18¾ ounces) **CAMPBELL'S Chunky Turkey Soup**
2 tablespoons water
1 tablespoon cornstarch
1 can (10 ounces) mandarin orange segments, drained
Cooked rice

In saucepan, cook celery and green pepper with garlic and ginger in butter until tender. Add soup. Blend water and cornstarch until smooth; stir into soup mixture. Cook, stirring until thickened. Add oranges; heat. Serve with rice.   *Makes about 3 cups*

Old-Fashioned Bread Stuffing

¾ cup finely chopped onion
¾ cup finely chopped celery
½ stick (¼ cup) butter or margarine
¾ teaspoon salt
¼ teaspoon poultry seasoning
¼ teaspoon sage
Pepper
4 cups dry bread cubes
2 tablespoons water

Cook onion and celery in butter until tender. Mix seasonings; sprinkle over bread cubes. Add onion mixture and water. Combine. Stuff thawed, rinsed turkey and roast immediately. *Yield: 4 cups (enough for 6 pound* **LI'L BUTTERBALL™ Turkey***)*

Note: 6 slices white bread = 5 cups soft bread cubes, dried overnight = 4½ cups dry bread cubes.

VARIATIONS:

Oyster Stuffing

Add 1 cup oysters, chopped, uncooked, or heated in butter, to Bread Stuffing.

Corn Bread Stuffing

Replace 4 cups bread cubes in Bread Stuffing with 4 cups crumbled corn bread. Combine as for Bread Stuffing.

Chestnut Stuffing

Add ½ cup chopped, cooked chestnuts.

Giblet Stuffing

Add cooked, cooled, chopped giblets to Bread Stuffing.

Fruited-Sausage Stuffing

1 pound bulk pork sausage
½ cup chopped celery
½ cup chopped onion
3 cups coarsely chopped fresh cranberries
1 can (8 ounces) undrained crushed pineapple
1½ cups water
1 package (8 ounces) **PEPPERIDGE FARM®** Herb
Seasoned Stuffing

In a skillet, brown pork sausage, stirring to break into bits. Add
celery and onion. Cook until tender, stirring frequently. Combine
with remaining ingredients. *Use to stuff 12 to 14 pound turkey*

Quick Turkey Stroganoff

2 lb. **JENNIE-O®** White, Dark, or **Combination Pan
Roast,** prepared according to pkg. directions
2 tablespoons butter or margarine
1 cup chopped onion
1 cup dairy sour cream
Cooked rice, egg noodles, or mashed potatoes

Cube turkey. Sauté onion in butter; stir in turkey. Prepare gravy
according to gravy packet directions; stir into turkey mixture. Add
sour cream; cook over low heat just until warm. Serve over hot
cooked rice, noodles, or mashed potatoes. *About 8 servings*

Turkey Breast á la Greque

1 package (4 to 5 lbs.) **LOUIS RICH™** Fresh Turkey
Breast Half
1 package (8 oz.) cream cheese, softened
1 can (3 oz.) real bacon bits
2 slices fresh bread, finely chopped
¼ cup chopped fresh parsley
1 teaspoon instant minced onion
½ teaspoon oregano
⅛ teaspoon garlic powder
1 egg, beaten

Rinse turkey and pat dry. With knife, loosen lining under skin, pulling skin back to expose meat. Leave skin attached along one edge. In large bowl combine remaining ingredients. Spread mixture on area where skin was removed. Replace skin; secure with poultry skewers or toothpicks. Place skin side up in shallow, foil-lined roasting pan. Insert meat thermometer into center of thickest part of muscle, taking care not to touch bone. Bake in 325°F oven 1½ hours. Baste with pan drippings; cover loosely with foil. Bake one hour longer until thermometer registers an internal temperature of 170°F. Remove from oven, let stand 10 minutes before slicing.   *Makes 8 to 10 servings*

Note: For 2 to 4 lb. breast half or portion, prepare as above. After basting and covering, bake 30 minutes more.

Spit-Roasted Duckling With Olive Barbecue Sauce

> 1 frozen duckling (4½ to 5 pounds), defrosted
> ½ teaspoon garlic salt
> ½ cup catsup
> ½ cup water
> ¼ cup chopped onion
> 3 tablespoons red wine vinegar
> 1 clove garlic, cut in half
> 1½ teaspoons sugar
> ¼ teaspoon paprika
> ½ cup sliced stuffed olives

Wash, drain and dry duckling. Sprinkle neck and body cavities with garlic salt. Skewer neck skin to back. Truss duckling compactly. Tie wings against breast. Tie legs together loosely, looping cord around tail. Insert rotisserie spit lengthwise through duck cavities on a slight angle; balance and tighten holding prongs. Roast on rotisserie over moderate to low heat until meat on drumstick is very tender, about 2½ hours. While duckling is roasting, prepare sauce. Combine catsup, water, onion, vinegar, garlic, sugar and paprika; simmer about 20 minutes. Remove garlic. Baste duckling with sauce frequently during last 30 minutes of roasting. Stir olives into remaining sauce; heat. Serve with duckling.   *Makes 3 to 4 servings*

Favorite recipe from the **National Duckling Council**

Fish

Red Snapper in Orange Sauce

2 lbs. **FIN BRAND Red Snapper**
3 Tbsp. orange juice
1 Tbsp. grated orange rind
5 Tbsp. butter or margarine (melted)
1 tsp. lemon juice
Salt and pepper to taste
Dash of nutmeg

Place fillets in a single layer in well-greased baking pan. Combine remaining ingredients and pour over fish. Bake in 350 degree F oven 25-30 minutes or until fish flakes easily when tested with a fork. Remove to warm serving platter, pour any sauce remaining in the pan over fish and garnish with parsley.

Poached Red Snapper With Lemons and Grapes

1 13 ounce Red Snapper (Cleaned and scaled with head/tail left on)
Lemons, peeled, pitted and thinly sliced
Grapes (Red or white, seedless)
¼ cup olive oil
⅛-¼ teaspoon salt
⅛-¼ teaspoon pepper
½ cup **CANADA DRY® Club Soda**

Preheat oven to 400°F. Place large pan, half filled with boiling water and grill rack in center of oven. Rub Snapper with oil and set aside. Combine lemons and grapes in medium-size bowl. Lightly salt and pepper Snapper. Place on grill and bake about 30 minutes. Add remaining oil and **CANADA DRY® Club Soda** to pan and simmer. Add lemons and grapes and heat to warm. Serve on a platter. Pour lemon/grape sauce over fish and garnish with parsley or dill. *Makes 2 Servings*

Flounder Nouvelle

3 tablespoons **MAZOLA® Corn Oil**, divided
1 cup chopped onions
1 clove garlic
¼ cup dry white wine
½ teaspoon salt
¾ pound flounder fillets (4 small)
3 medium carrots, cut in match-stick pieces
3 ribs celery, cut in match-stick pieces

In medium skillet heat 1 tablespoon of the corn oil over medium heat. Add onion and garlic. Cook, stirring frequently, 5 minutes. Place onion mixture, wine and salt in blender container; cover. Blend on high speed 15 seconds or until smooth. Beginning with tail end roll each flounder fillet lengthwise; place in 1-quart shallow baking pan. Spoon onion mixture over fish. Bake uncovered in 375°F oven 20 minutes. Meanwhile, heat remaining 2 tablespoons of the corn oil in skillet over medium heat. Add carrots and celery. Cook, stirring frequently, 5 minutes. Spoon over fish. Bake 5 minutes longer or until fish flakes easily.

Makes 4 servings

MICROWAVE METHOD:
In 2-quart microproof bowl place 1 tablespoon of the corn oil, onions and garlic. Microwave with full power 2 minutes, stirring once. Place onion mixture, wine and salt in blender container: cover. Blend on high speed 10 seconds or until pureed. In 2-quart microproof bowl place remaining 2 tablespoons corn oil, carrots and celery. Microwave 2½ minutes, stirring once. Beginning with tail end roll each flounder fillet lengthwise; place in 8 × 8 × 2-inch microproof baking dish. Spoon onion mixture over fish; top with carrot and celery mixture. Cover with waxed paper. Microwave 7 to 8 minutes rotating dish twice or until fish flakes easily.

Makes 4 servings

Sole Amandine

1 - 14 oz. pkg. **HIGH LINER® Sole Fillets**
¾ cup blanched almonds
6 Tbsp. butter
Flour
Salt
Pepper

Melt butter in skillet over medium high heat. Dust frozen fish with flour and season to taste with salt and pepper. Place in skillet. Cut ¼ cup of almonds into slivers, leaving the remainder whole. Sprinkle almonds in pan around fish, stirring them to prevent burning. Turn fish once while frying. Fry approximately 6-8 minutes each side. To serve, pour almond butter over fish. Garnish with parsley and lemon wedges.   *Serves 3-4*

Mushroom-Sole Crêpes
au Gratin

1 can (3 oz.) **BinB® Sliced Mushrooms,**
    drained—reserving broth
1 lb. fillet of sole, cut in 1-inch strips
1 package (10 oz.) frozen chopped spinach, thawed and
    drained
2 tablespoons dry white wine
1 teaspoon lemon juice
Salt and pepper to taste
2 tablespoons butter or margarine
2 tablespoons flour
½ cup minced green onion
Milk
½ cup shredded Swiss cheese
½ cup shredded cheddar cheese
8 crêpes (use favorite recipe)

Wipe fish dry, place in shallow baking dish. Cover with wine, lemon juice and seasonings. In a saucepan, melt butter or margarine and sauté onions until tender; blend in flour. Add enough milk to broth to make 1¼ cups. Add cheese and cook over low heat until cheese is melted, stirring constantly. Pour off ½ cup and fold into fish and spinach. Add mushrooms to remaining sauce. Divide fish-spinach mixture into eighths. Fill each crepe and roll. Place in oiled shallow baking dish. Cover and heat in 350°F. oven for 20 minutes. For each serving, use two crepes and top with warm mushroom sauce.   *Makes 4 to 6 servings*

Chile Stuffed Fillet of Sole

1 small onion, chopped
2 tablespoons butter (or margarine)
1 cup fresh bread crumbs
1 can (4 oz.) **ORTEGA Diced Green Chiles**
1 egg, lightly beaten
Salt and pepper to taste
6 fillets of sole (approximately 2 lbs.)
1 can (10½ oz.) condensed Cheddar cheese soup

Sauté onion in butter. In a bowl, mix bread crumbs, chiles, and onion. Stir in egg and salt and pepper. Spread some of this mixture evenly over each fillet, roll and fasten each with a toothpick. Set, seam side down, in well-greased 6″ x 9″ x 2″ baking pan. Bake, uncovered, in preheated oven (350°) for 15 minutes. Drain excess liquid. Spoon undiluted soup over fillets and continue baking for 15 minutes, or until fish flakes. Serve hot.   *Serves 6*

Honey Barbecued
Farm-Raised Catfish

4 pan-dressed **FARM-RAISED CATFISH** (10 to 12
 ounces) fresh or frozen
2 tablespoons cornstarch or flour

Sauce:

1 cup tomato catsup
3 tablespoons unsalted butter or margarine
3 tablespoons finely chopped green onion
2 tablespoons lemon juice
2 tablespoons Worcestershire sauce
1 tablespoon honey
1 tablespoon pineapple preserves
⅛ teaspoon garlic juice
⅛ teaspoon liquid hot pepper sauce
⅛ teaspoon charcoal seasoning (optional)

4 slices pineapple
2 cans (16 ounces each) white whole kernel corn
2 tablespoons melted butter or margarine
Red onion rings
Lemon wedges

Thaw fish if frozen. Score fish on both sides, diamond shaped, making cuts approximately 1 inch apart. Dust fish with cornstarch. Place fish on a well-greased broiler pan.

SAUCE:

In a saucepan, combine catsup, 3 tablespoons butter, green onion, lemon juice, Worcestershire sauce, honey, preserves, garlic juice, liquid hot pepper sauce and charcoal seasoning, if used. Bring mixture to a boil, stirring constantly; simmer for 10 minutes.

Brush fish liberally with sauce, making sure sauce gets into scored sections. Broil approximately 6 inches from source of heat for 8 minutes. Turn fish and brush fish with sauce. Place pineapple rings on broiler pan with fish. Continue to broil another 8 minutes or until fish is opaque and flakes easily when tested with a fork and pineapple is slightly browned.

While fish is broiling heat corn. Drain liquid from corn and stir in 2 tablespoons melted butter. Spread corn over bottom of a warm shallow platter, building up sides slightly. Line the catfish down the center, flanking with 2 pineapple slices on either end. If desired, spoon remaining heated sauce over the catfish only or serve with just the entrée. Garnish with red onion rings and lemon wedges. *Makes four servings*

Note: When eating, use lemon juice squeezed from wedges to taste.

Favorite recipe from the **Catfish Farmers of America**

Baked Whole Fish With Mushrooms

3½ pounds whole striped bass, rainbow trout or red
  snapper
Flour
Salt and pepper
3 tablespoons **BERTOLLI**® Olive Oil
2 tablespoons butter
1 rib celery, thinly sliced
1 medium carrot, thinly sliced
8 ounces mushrooms, thinly sliced
¼ cup minced parsley
2 tablespoons **BERTOLLI**® Orvieto Wine
¼ teaspoon each salt and pepper
1⅓ cups **BERTOLLI**® Spaghetti Sauce With
  Mushrooms
¼ cup sliced green onions
Lemon wedges

Coat fish with flour; sprinkle with salt and pepper. Sauté in oil and butter in large skillet until brown; remove. Sauté vegetables, except green onions, wine, salt and pepper 5 minutes. Spread ⅔ vegetables on oven-proof platter; spoon ⅔ cup sauce over. Stuff fish with remaining vegetables; arrange on platter. Spoon remaining sauce on fish; bake at 425° until fish is tender, about 20 minutes. Sprinkle with onions; garnish with lemon.

Makes 4-6 servings

Baked Haddock in Cucumber Sauce

2 pounds frozen haddock fillets, thawed
2 tablespoons **MEADOW GOLD® Butter**, melted
¼ teaspoon salt
⅛ teaspoon each: pepper, paprika
¼ cup sliced green onions
¼ cup (½ stick) **MEADOW GOLD® Butter**
¼ cup flour
1 teaspoon salt
1 container (8 ounces) **MEADOW GOLD® Plain Lowfat Yogurt**
1 cup chopped, pared cucumber, drained

Pat fillets dry with paper toweling; arrange in shallow baking dish. Brush with melted butter; sprinkle with ¼ teaspoon salt, pepper and paprika. Cook onions in ¼ cup butter for 2 to 3 minutes. Remove from heat. Add flour and salt; mix well. Stir in yogurt. Cook, stirring constantly, until mixture begins to boil. Stir in cucumber. Spoon sauce over fillets. Bake at 350° for 30 minutes, or until hot and bubbly.   *6 to 8 servings*

Lemon Delight Fish Fillets

4 sole or haddock fillets (about 1 pound)
Salt and pepper
2 tablespoons fresh squeezed lemon juice
Fine dry bread crumbs (seasoned or plain)
2 tablespoons butter or margarine
2 tablespoons salad oil
⅓ cup light cream or half & half
1 teaspoon fresh grated lemon peel
1 avocado, sliced
Whole or chopped salted cashew nuts
SUNKIST® Lemon, cut in half-cartwheels
Parsley

Sprinkle fillets with salt, pepper and 1 tablespoon lemon juice; let stand 5 to 10 minutes. Coat fillets with bread crumbs. In large skillet, heat butter and oil. Sauté fillets (3 to 4 minutes on each side) until lightly browned and fish flakes easily with fork. Remove fillets to serving dish; sprinkle with remaining 1 tablespoon lemon juice. Keep warm. Add cream and lemon peel to pan drippings. Bring to boil, stirring constantly until slightly thickened; spoon over fillets. Top with avocado slices and nuts. Serve with lemon half-cartwheels. Garnish with parsley.

Makes 4 servings

Lemon Buttered Fish

¼ cup margarine or butter
¼ cup **REALEMON® Reconstituted Lemon Juice**
¼ cup water
1 teaspoon **WYLER'S® Chicken-Flavor Instant Bouillon** *or* 1 **WYLER'S® Chicken-Flavor Bouillon Cube**
¼ teaspoon thyme leaves or dill weed
1 pound fish fillets, fresh or frozen, thawed (turbot, sole, perch, haddock, salmon or flounder)
Salt and pepper
Paprika

In large skillet, combine margarine, **REALEMON®**, water, bouillon and thyme; heat until margarine is melted and bouillon is dissolved. Add fish; cover and simmer 6 to 8 minutes or until fish flakes with fork. Season with salt and pepper; garnish with paprika. Refrigerate leftovers.

Makes 3 to 4 servings

Flounder Caribe

1 pound **BOOTH Flounder Fillets**
1-10½ oz. can condensed tomato soup
⅓ cup diced green pepper
¼ cup diced onion
¼ teaspoon thyme
1 teaspoon Worcestershire sauce
2 tablespoons white wine

Defrost fillets. Roll up and place in a single layer in a buttered baking dish. Combine tomato soup (undiluted), green pepper, onion, thyme, Worcestershire sauce and white wine. Pour over fish and bake in a preheated 350°F oven 20-25 minutes, until fish flakes easily with a fork.

Eatwell®
Mackerel Loaf

1 can **EATWELL® Mackerel**
¾ cup bread crumbs
¾ cup milk
½ cup coarsely chopped gherkins or pickle relish
2 eggs
1½ teaspoons salt
1½ Tbsp. melted butter or margarine

1 teaspoon minced onion
1½ cups medium white sauce
2 hard cooked eggs, sliced
6 stuffed olives, sliced

Flake mackerel. Add crumbs, milk, gherkins, eggs, salt and melted butter or margarine. Mix well. Pack into greased loaf pan. Set in shallow pan of hot water and bake in moderate oven (350°) about 30 minutes or until loaf becomes firm. Turn out on hot platter. Add onion to white sauce and pour over loaf. Arrange egg slices on top with an olive slice on top of each.

Fish Creole

1 can (8 oz.) stewed tomatoes
1 teaspoon **KITCHEN BOUQUET**®
¼ teaspoon sugar
¼ teaspoon thyme, crumbled
¼ teaspoon curry powder
1 lb. fresh or thawed frozen white fish
Salt to taste
Parsley (optional)

Combine tomatoes, **KITCHEN BOUQUET**®, sugar, thyme and curry powder, breaking up large tomato pieces with spoon. Cut fish into 4 portions. Place in shallow baking pan. Spoon tomato mixture over top. Cover pan with lid or foil. Bake in 450° oven for 15 minutes or until fish flakes with fork. Sprinkle with minced parsley, if desired. Salt to taste. Serve with rice, spooning pan juices over. Cooking time: 15 minutes. *Makes 4 servings*

Fish Fillets Paprikash

1 package (14 ounces) **MRS. PAUL'S**® **French Fried
    Fish Fillets**
3 tablespoons butter or margarine
¼ cup onions, diced
1 tablespoon flour
1 teaspoon paprika
1 cup milk
¾ cup sour cream
½ teaspoon salt
½ teaspoon parsley flakes
1 package (8 ounces) egg noodles, cooked according to
    package directions

Prepare **MRS. PAUL'S**® **French Fried Fish Fillets** according to package directions. Sauté onion in butter over medium heat until soft. Stir in flour and paprika and cook over low heat for 2-3 minutes. Gradually add milk and salt, heat until thickened. Remove from heat and stir in sour cream. Place noodles on serving dish. Arrange fish fillets on noodles and spoon sauce over fish fillets. Garnish with parsley flakes. *Serves 6*

Greek Fillets
(Ocean Perch)

1 lb. BOOTH Block Frozen Fillets
1 tablespoon softened butter or margarine

Let fillets stand at room temperature 30 minutes. Cut into four equal portions and place on greased aluminum foil. Spread softened butter or margarine on fish and wrap securely. Bake 30-35 minutes at 450°F. or until fish flakes easily with a fork. While fish is baking prepare sauce.

Greek Sauce

1 cup sliced celery
½ cup minced onion
¼ cup butter or margarine (or combination of half olive oil and half butter or margarine)
1 can (16 oz.) stewed tomatoes, cut up
1 can (3.2 oz.) sliced ripe olives, drained
¼ teaspoon garlic powder
3-4 drops liquid hot pepper sauce
2-3 tablespoons white wine (optional)
¾ cup Feta cheese, crumbled

Melt butter or margarine; sauté celery and onion. Add tomatoes and liquid and rest of ingredients except cheese. Simmer 10-15 minutes. Just before serving, remove sauce from heat and blend in Feta cheese. Serve immediately over steamed fillets.

Serves 3-4

Beer Batter Fish

1 pound fish fillets or cooked large shrimp
3 to 4 tablespoons BISQUICK® Baking Mix
1 cup BISQUICK® Baking Mix
½ cup beer
1 egg
½ teaspoon salt
Soy sauce or vinegar

Heat fat or oil (1½ inches) in heavy saucepan or deep-fat fryer to 350°. Lightly coat fish with 3 to 4 tablespoons baking mix; reserve. Mix 1 cup baking mix. the beer, egg and salt until smooth. Dip fish into batter, letting excess drip into bowl. Fry fish until golden brown, about 2 minutes on each side; drain. Serve hot with soy sauce.   *3 or 4 servings*

Fish Sticks With Sour Cream and Mushrooms

1 package (14 ounces) **MRS. PAUL'S® French Fried Fish Sticks**
3 tablespoons butter or margarine
1 cup mushrooms, sliced
¼ cup onion, diced
1 tablespoon parsley flakes
Pinch of black pepper
¼ teaspoon paprika
⅛ teaspoon garlic powder
1 can (10¾ ounces) condensed cream of mushroom soup
¼ cup milk
1 cup sour cream
1½ teaspoons sherry cooking wine or water
3 cups cooked rice or noodles, prepared according to package directions

Prepare 1 package (14 ounces) **MRS. PAUL'S® French Fried Fish Sticks** according to package directions. Meanwhile, melt butter in medium saucepan over medium-low heat. Add mushrooms, onion, parsley, pepper, paprika, and garlic powder, then sauté for approximately 5 minutes. Blend soup, milk, sour cream and sherry in small bowl. Gradually add to sautéed mushrooms and heat over low heat until thickened. Place rice on serving platter and arrange fish sticks on top. Spoon sauce over fish sticks and serve.   *Serves 6*

Land O' Lakes Classic Salmon Steaks
(Low Sodium)

Topping:
½ cup **LAND O LAKES® Unsalted (Sweet) Butter**, softened
1 tsp. lime juice
¼ tsp. dill weed
⅛ tsp. pepper

4 salmon steaks (1" thick)
1 lime, cut into 8 slices

Combine all topping ingredients until well blended. Place salmon steaks on greased broiler pan. Spread one side of each steak with 2 tsp. topping. Broil 5" away from heat for 5 to 6 min. or until lightly browned. Turn steaks over and top each steak with 2 lime slices. Continue broiling 5 to 6 min. or until salmon flakes with fork. To serve, place lime slices beside steak and top each steak with 1 Tbsp. topping.   *Yield: 4 servings*

Sodium: 153 mg/serving

Salmon in Potato Shells
(Low Calorie)

	Calories
1-15½ oz. can **HUMPTY DUMPTY Chum Salmon***	554
3 large baking potatoes (approx. 8 oz. ea.)	418
½ cup skim milk	45
1 teaspoon dried dill weed	—
1 teaspoon garlic salt	—
¼ teaspoon pepper	—
Paprika	—
	1017

Drain salmon and flake. Bake potatoes as usual; cool slightly. Cut in half lengthwise and scoop out cooked potato, leaving shell intact. Beat cooked potato with skim milk until fluffy; add more milk if necessary. Stir in salmon, dill, garlic salt and pepper. Spoon into potato shells and sprinkle with paprika. Return to hot oven and bake until heated through.   *Makes 6 servings*

Calories per half = Approx. 169

*DEMING'S, **DOUBLE Q** or **GILLNETTERSBEST Salmon** may be substituted.

Salmon Stuffed Green Peppers
(Low Calorie)

	Calories
1-15½ oz. can **DOUBLE Q Pink Salmon***	554
6 medium green peppers	78
⅔ cup chopped green onion	30
1½ cups cooked enriched rice	300
½ cup low fat cottage cheese	100
2 tablespoons lemon juice	8
Salt and pepper to taste	—
1-15 oz. can tomato sauce	170
	1240

Drain salmon and flake. Cut peppers in half lengthwise; remove stems, pulp and seeds. Parboil in salted water for 2-3 minutes or until slightly tender; invert on paper towel to drain. Mix together salmon, green onions, rice, cottage cheese, lemon juice and ½ cup of tomato sauce. Season to taste with salt and pepper. Fill pepper shells with salmon mixture and place in baking pan. Top with remaining tomato sauce. Bake in 400° oven for 15-20 minutes or until peppers are heated through.   *Makes 6 servings*

Calories per serving = 206 (2 pepper halves)

*DEMING'S, **GILLNETTERSBEST** or **HUMPTY DUMPTY Salmon** may be substituted.

Salmon a la King With Spinach Noodles

3 quarts water
3 teaspoons salt
1 tablespoon oil
4 cups **AMERICAN BEAUTY®** Spinach Egg Noodles
  or 6 cups **Extra Wide Egg Noodles**
1 tablespoon chopped onion
1 tablespoon margarine or butter
⅓ cup flour
1 teaspoon salt
Dash pepper
3 cups milk
1 tablespoon chopped pimiento
7¾-oz. can salmon
3 hard-cooked eggs, sliced

Boil water in large deep pot with 3 teaspoons salt and oil (to prevent boiling over). Add noodles; stir to separate. Cook uncovered after water returns to a full rolling boil for 6 to 7 minutes. Stir occasionally. Drain and rinse under hot water.

In large saucepan, cook onion in margarine until tender. Stir in flour, salt and pepper until well blended. Add milk all at once. Cook until thickened, stirring constantly. Stir in pimiento, salmon and eggs; cook until heated through. Serve over cooked spinach egg noodles.   *6 servings*

High Altitude—Above 3500 Feet: Cooking times may need to be increased slightly for noodles.

NUTRITION INFORMATION PER SERVING
SERVING SIZE: ⅙ of recipe

		Percent U.S. RDA	
Calories	620	Per Serving	
Protein	28	Protein	42
Carbohydrate	80	Vitamin A	17
Fat	20	Vitamin C	2
Sodium	670	Thiamine	35
Potassium	485	Riboflavin	35
		Niacin	34
		Calcium	25
		Iron	21

Tuna
Croquettes

3 tablespoons CRISCO® Shortening
¼ cup flour
⅔ cup milk
2 tablespoons finely chopped onion
1 tablespoon snipped parsley
2 teaspoons lemon juice
¼ teaspoon salt
Dash pepper
Dash paprika
2 cans (6¼ or 7 ounces each) tuna, drained and flaked
⅔ cup fine dry bread crumbs
1 egg, beaten
1 package (8 ounces) frozen peas with cream sauce
CRISCO® Shortening for deep frying

In saucepan, melt the 3 tablespoons **CRISCO®**. Blend in the flour. Add the milk. Cook and stir till thickened and bubbly. Add the onion, parsley, lemon juice, salt, pepper, and paprika; stir in the tuna. Cover and chill thoroughly, about 3 hours. With wet hands, shape tuna mixture into 8 cones, using about ¼ cup for each. Roll in crumbs. Dip into a mixture of beaten egg and **2 tablespoons water**; roll in crumbs again. Prepare peas with cream sauce according to package directions; keep hot. Meanwhile, fry a few croquettes at a time in deep **CRISCO®** heated to 350° till brown and hot, about 3 minutes. Drain on paper toweling. Spoon pea sauce over croquettes. *Makes 4 servings*

Tuna Veracruz

1½ tablespoons olive oil
1 clove garlic, minced
1 onion, thinly sliced
1 can (1 pound) whole tomatoes, drained, crushed
1 tablespoon tomato paste
1 small bay leaf
¼ teaspoon dry oregano
10 green olives with pimiento, cut in half
1 tablespoon capers
4 ounces canned whole green chilies, cut in strips
½ teaspoon hot pepper sauce
2 tablespoons lemon juice
1 12½ or 13 ounce can **CHICKEN OF THE SEA®**
   Tuna, drained
4 cups cooked white rice

Pour olive oil into heavy 12 inch skillet. Sauté garlic and onions over moderate heat for 3 to 5 minutes. Add tomatoes, tomato paste (freeze leftover tomato paste for future use), bay leaf, oregano, olives, capers, chilies, hot pepper sauce, and lemon juice.

Cook, stirring, over moderate heat for 15 minutes or until mixture is thick and some of the liquid has evaporated. Add tuna and heat thoroughly.

Prepare rice according to package directions. Serve at once, or refrigerate and reheat before serving. *Serves 4*

Oriental
Sweet and Sour Tuna

1 8-ounce can pineapple chunks, packed in natural juice
1 tablespoon cornstarch
¼ teaspoon salt
¼ cup cider vinegar
2 tablespoons **SWEETLITE**™ **Fructose**
2 teaspoons soy sauce
½ cup sliced fresh mushrooms
½ bell pepper thinly sliced
½ onion thinly sliced
1 6-ounce can water chestnuts, drained and thinly sliced
2 7-ounce cans white tuna packed in water, drained
2 cups cooked rice

Drain the juice from the pineapple chunks and pour it in a large saucepan. Add the cornstarch, salt and vinegar and stir until the cornstarch is completely dissolved. Place the pan on medium heat and cook, stirring constantly, until the sauce has thickened. Add all other ingredients except the tuna and cooked rice. Cook until the vegetables are done but still crisp—about 5 minutes. Break the tuna into bite sized chunks and add it to the other ingredients. Mix well and serve each portion over ½ cup of the cooked rice.

Makes 4 servings

Shellfish

Batter-Fried Shrimp

2 eggs
½ cup milk
1 cup all-purpose flour, stirred before measuring
1 teaspoon baking powder
1 teaspoon salt
2 teaspoons cooking oil
2 pounds fresh or frozen whole shrimp
Oil or shortening for deep-fat frying
Orange Sauce (recipe follows)
Grape-Horseradish Sauce (recipe follows)
Plum Hot (recipe follows)

Beat together eggs and milk until frothy. Sift together flour, baking powder, and salt. Add to egg mixture; add oil and beat until mixture is smooth and well-blended. Set aside. Remove shells from shrimp, leaving tails on. If shrimp are frozen, remove shells under running cold water. Cut partway through lengthwise along outside curve. Lift out vein; wash shrimp and flatten so they stay open. Drain well on paper towels. Place enough oil or shortening to more than cover shrimp in a deep-fat fryer or kettle and heat to 375°F. Dip shrimp into batter, one at a time, and fry, a few at a time, about 4 minutes, or until golden brown and puffy. Drain on paper towels. Serve immediately with Orange Sauce, Grape-Horseradish Sauce, or Plum Hot.   *Makes 6 servings*

Orange Sauce

1 cup **SMUCKER'S Sweet Orange Marmalade**
1 clove garlic
1 piece whole ginger root or ½ teaspoon ground ginger

In a saucepan, combine all ingredients and cook over low heat, stirring constantly, until mixture bubbles. Remove garlic and ginger root.   *Makes about 1 cup*

Grape-Horseradish Sauce

1 cup **SMUCKER'S Grape Jelly**
1 tablespoon prepared horseradish
¼ cup ketchup

Combine all ingredients.   *Makes about 1 cup*

Plum Hot

1 cup **SMUCKER'S Plum Preserves**
1 to 2 cloves garlic, as desired, very finely minced
2 teaspoons soy sauce
¼ teaspoon pepper

In a saucepan, combine all ingredients and cook over low heat, stirring occasionally, at least 5 minutes, or until garlic is cooked. Remove from heat and cool slightly.   *Makes about 1 cup*

Coconut
Fried Shrimp

1 lb. small raw shrimp, shelled and deveined
⅓ cup lemon juice
½ tsp. salt
⅓ tsp. ground ginger
3 tsp. curry powder
1¾ cups flour
2 tsp. baking powder
1¼ cups skimmed milk
½ cup **COCO CASA™ Cream of Coconut**
3½ oz. can flaked coconut
Fat for frying

Marinate shrimp in lemon juice, salt, ginger and curry powder for 1 to 2 hours. Drain well. Prepare batter of 1½ cups flour, baking powder, milk and Cream of Coconut. Coat shrimp with remaining flour; dip in prepared batter and then dip lightly into flaked coconut. Fry in deep fat (hot) about 2-3 minutes. Fry only about 6 shrimp at a time.

Heart's Delight Shrimp

1 15½ oz. can pineapple chunks or slices cut up
1 large green pepper
4 tablespoons butter
1 1-pound package **BORDO Whole Imported Dates**
1½ pounds cooked, shelled, deveined shrimp

Sauce:

1 cup pineapple juice
¼ teaspoon dry mustard
½ teaspoon ground ginger
¼ cup brown sugar
1 tablespoon cornstarch

Top:

2 tablespoons butter
½ cup dry bread crumbs

Drain pineapple, reserve liquid for sauce. Seed green pepper and slice into ¼ inch strips. Melt butter in large skillet. Sauté green pepper until it just begins to soften, about 2 minutes. Add pineapple chunks and dates and heat through, carefully mixing. Remove mixture from pan with slotted spoon and place in large bowl. Place shrimp in skillet and sauté 2-3 minutes. Mix shrimp with date mixture and place in 1½ quart casserole.

Sauce: In small saucepan, put 1 cup reserved pineapple juice (add water if necessary to make 1 cup). Add mustard, ginger and brown sugar and mix well. Blend small amount of water with cornstarch to dissolve, add to pineapple juice. Place over medium heat and cook until thick and clear, stirring constantly. Pour mixture over shrimp in casserole.

Top: Melt 2 tablespoons butter in skillet. Add bread crumbs and mix until moistened. Sprinkle over shrimp.

Bake at 350° for 25 minutes. Let stand 10 minutes before serving. *6 generous portions*

Shrimporee Creole

1 pound cooked shrimp, shelled, deveined
3 tablespoons butter or margarine
½ cup chopped onion
½ cup chopped green pepper
¼ cup minced celery
2 cloves garlic, minced
1 tablespoon flour
1 (1 pound) can sliced stewed tomatoes
⅛ teaspoon dried thyme
1 bay leaf
½ teaspoon **IMPERIAL Granulated Sugar**
Dash hot pepper sauce
1 teaspoon Worcestershire sauce
Several whole allspice
Salt and pepper
Minced parsley
Hot, freshly cooked rice

Cook shrimp. Remove shells. To make creole sauce, sauté onion, green pepper, garlic and celery in butter or margarine until limp; add flour and cook and stir until flour is light tan. Add all other ingredients except parsley and rice and cook until sauce is thickened. Taste for salt and pepper and add more if needed. Stir in parsley. Serve over hot, freshly cooked rice. *Serves 4*

Shrimp Creole

2 Tbsp. butter or margarine
¾ cup chopped onion
½ cup chopped green pepper
¼ cup chopped celery
1 6-oz. can tomato paste
2 cups water
2-3 tsp. **BALTIMORE SPICE OLD BAY Seasoning,**
     depending on heat preference
1 tsp. salt
1 bay leaf, whole or crushed
2 cups cleaned cooked shrimp
3 cups hot cooked rice or spaghetti

In 10″ skillet sauté onion and green pepper in butter until tender. Stir in remaining ingredients except shrimp and rice or spaghetti. Cook over low heat stirring occasionally, about 20 minutes. Stir in shrimp; heat through about 5-8 minutes. Serve over rice or spaghetti.   *6 servings*

Curried Shrimp With Apples

4 Tbsp. butter (or margarine)
1½ cups **LUCKY LEAF® Sliced Apples**
3 or 4 tsp. curry powder
¼ cup flour
3¾ cups milk
2 tsp. salt
4 cups cooked, cleaned shrimp (2 lbs. in shell)
5 cups hot cooked rice
Paprika

Melt butter in skillet. Add coarsely diced apples and simmer a few minutes. Mix flour and curry powder and stir into apples. Slowly add milk. Cook while stirring until thick. Add salt and shrimp and heat slowly. Serve with hot fluffy rice sprinkled with paprika.

Serves 8

Shrimp Teriyaki

2 lbs. ATALANTA Frozen Shrimp, raw, shelled, deveined
1 cup Pineapple Juice
6 Tbsp. Soy Sauce
½ cup Vegetable Oil

Marinate shrimp in juice, soy sauce and oil for 20 minutes. Drain and broil shrimps 4 minutes on each side. Serve with rice.

Yield: 6 servings

Elegant Chicken and Shrimp

¼ cup butter or margarine
8 oz. sliced fresh mushrooms
¼ cup sliced green onions
2 Tbsp. unsifted all purpose flour
1 cup half-and-half
2 Tbsp. dry sherry
1 cup **KAUKAUNA® Cheese Sharp Cheddar Buttery Spread**™
2 cups cubed, cooked chicken
1 cup cooked shrimp
2 Tbsp. snipped fresh parsley
2 Tbsp. diced pimiento
Hot cooked rice

Melt butter in large skillet. Add mushrooms and green onions. Sauté over low heat until tender. Blend in flour until smooth. Add half-and-half and sherry. Stir constantly until mixture boils and thickens. Stir in cheese until melted. Blend in chicken and shrimp. Heat to serving temperature. Stir in parsley and pimiento before serving. Serve over hot cooked rice.   *Makes 4-5 servings*

Shrimp Elegant

3 tablespoons butter or margarine
⅓ cup finely chopped onion
1 garlic clove, minced
1 small can sliced mushrooms, drained
½ cup chopped green pepper
1 pound **BOOTH Peeled and Deveined Shrimp**, frozen
1-10½ oz. can condensed cheddar cheese soup
⅓ cup half-and-half
¼ cup dry sherry

Melt butter in large saucepan; sauté onion, garlic, mushrooms and green pepper until tender but not brown, about 5 minutes. Add shrimp and sauté another 5-7 minutes. Drain off liquid. Stir in soup; gradually blend in half-and-half and wine. Cook, stirring occasionally until heated through. Serve over rice.

Baked Squash With Seafood Stuffing

2 small acorn squash
3 Tbsp. margarine
¾ cup finely chopped celery
3 Tbsp. finely chopped onions
¾ cup crab, shrimp or tuna (drain if canned)
½ tsp. salt
¼ tsp. pepper
½ tsp. Worcestershire sauce
2 cups **ROMAN MEAL® Bread Cubes** (3 to 4 slices)
¾ cup (3 oz.) grated Cheddar cheese

Clean squash. Cut in half; remove seeds and strings. Brush 1 Tbsp. of the margarine over bottom of 9 × 9 × 2-inch baking dish. Place squash, cut side down, in dish. Cover; bake until tender in moderate oven (375°) about 30 minutes. Meanwhile, sauté celery and onion in remaining margarine until tender. In medium bowl combine seafood, salt, pepper, Worcestershire, bread and ¼ cup of the cheese. When squash is tender, scoop meat out of shell; mash and season with ½ tsp. salt, ¼ tsp. pepper and 1 Tbsp. milk. Line shells with mashed squash. Place ¾ cup stuffing in each squash half; top with remaining cheese. Return to baking dish cut side up. Cover; bake at 350° F. about 25 minutes.

High Liner® Seafood Crêpes

Crêpes:
¾ cup flour
1 Tbsp. sugar
½ tsp. salt
3 eggs
1 cup milk
1 Tbsp. melted butter

Beat eggs until just blended in large bowl. Sift flour, sugar, salt over eggs and beat in, just until smooth. Stir in milk and melted butter. Heat 8 inch fry pan and grease lightly. Pour ⅓ cup batter in; tilting pan to cover bottom. Cook 1-2 minutes—turn and cook 1 minute longer. Roll up and place on cookie sheet. Keep warm. Repeat with remaining batter, greasing pan before each.

Crêpes Filling:
1 - 16 oz. pkg. **HIGH LINER® Fillets**, cooked and flaked
1 - 12 oz. pkg. **HIGH LINER® Frozen Shrimp**, cooked
1 pkg. broccoli spears, cooked
⅓ cup onion, finely chopped
2 Tbsp. butter
3 Tbsp. flour
2 cups milk
¾ cup shredded Swiss cheese
⅓ cup grated Parmesan cheese
⅓ cup dry white wine
Slivered almonds

Sauté onions in butter. Blend in flour. Add milk, stirring constantly over medium heat until thickened. Add Swiss and Parmesan cheese. Stir until melted and add wine. To ½ cup sauce, gently fold in fillets and shrimp. Unroll crêpes. On each crêpe place 2 broccoli spears, with flowered ends protruding. Add 2 heaping tablespoons sauce mixture and re-roll. Place on lightly greased baking dish. Pour remaining sauce over all the rolled crêpes and sprinkle with almonds. Bake in 350°F oven for 30 minutes.

Serves 6-8

Scallops au Gratin

4 BAYS® English Muffins
1 pound scallops (sliced in half)
1 cup chicken stock
4 tablespoons salted butter
¼ cup chopped green pepper
¼ cup chopped onion
¼ teaspoon paprika
3 tablespoons all-purpose flour
1 cup whipping cream
1 pimiento, chopped (approx. ¼ cup)
2 tablespoons sherry
¼ teaspoon salt
Dash pepper
Dash nutmeg
Parmesan cheese
Bread crumbs
Butter

Put scallops and chicken stock in a large frying pan and poach until scallops are opaque. Remove scallops. Reserve 1 cup of the poaching liquid. In the same frying pan, melt butter and sauté green pepper and onion, over low heat, until soft. Turn up heat to medium; stir in paprika and flour. Stir constantly for about 1 minute. Take pan off heat and stir in reserved poaching liquid and cream. Return pan to the heat and stir constantly until mixture thickens and comes to a full boil. Add pimientos, sherry, salt, pepper and nutmeg. Stir well. Fold in cooked scallops. Keep mixture warm. Toast and lightly butter 4 **BAYS® English Muffins**. Place two halves in each of four au gratin dishes. Pour ⅔ cup of the scallop mixture in each dish. Sprinkle with parmesan cheese and bread crumbs. Dot with butter. Broil until lightly browned and bubbly. Serve immediately.   *serves 4*

Crab Filled Crepes

1 (6-oz.) pkg. **WAKEFIELD**® **Crabmeat**
¼ cup butter or margarine
⅓ cup chopped green onions
1 cup thinly sliced celery
1 cup chopped mushrooms
3 tablespoons flour
1⅓ cups milk
⅓ cup grated Swiss cheese
¼ teaspoon salt
⅛ teaspoon pepper
Dash nutmeg
8 cooked crepes
Parmesan cheese (optional)

Thaw crabmeat, retain liquid and separate into chunks. In saucepan sauté onions, celery and mushrooms in butter or margarine for 2 to 3 minutes. Remove with slotted spoon and set aside. Stir flour into fat until smooth. Add milk and crab liquid, cook until thickened. Stir in cheese, salt, pepper and nutmeg. In small bowl toss together crab, onions, celery, mushrooms and ½ cup of sauce. Season to taste. Spread equal amount of filling across center of each crepe and roll up or fold over. Place in shallow baking pan and pour remaining sauce over the top. Sprinkle with Parmesan cheese if desired. Heat in 350° oven for 10 to 15 minutes.

Makes 8 crepes

Pasta

Noodles Primavera

½ (12-oz.) pkg. **AMERICAN BEAUTY® Wide Egg Noodles**
¼ cup butter or margarine
1 clove garlic, minced
1 cup chopped onions
1 cup thinly sliced carrots
1 cup frozen peas
1 small bunch fresh broccoli, cut into 1-inch pieces, or 10-oz. pkg. frozen chopped broccoli, thawed and drained
4½-oz. or 2 (2½-oz.) jars **GREEN GIANT® Whole Mushrooms**, drained
½ teaspoon basil leaves
¼ teaspoon seasoned salt
1 medium zucchini, cut into 1½-inch lengths and quartered
Grated Parmesan cheese

Cook noodles to desired doneness as directed on package. In large skillet, melt butter over low heat. Stir in garlic and onions; sauté for 2 minutes. Add remaining ingredients except zucchini and parmesan cheese; sauté until tender-crisp, about 5 minutes, stirring occasionally. Add zucchini; sauté an additional 5 minutes. Combine cooked noodles and vegetables; toss lightly. If desired, sprinkle with Parmesan cheese.   *8 (1-cup) servings*

HIGH ALTITUDE—Above 3500 feet: Cooking time may need to be increased slightly for noodles.

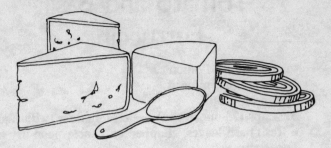

Fettuccine Alla Papalina

¼ cup butter or margarine
½ pound fresh mushrooms, sliced, or 1 can (8 ounces)
   sliced mushrooms, drained
1 cup chopped onion
1 pound cooked ham, diced
1 recipe White Sauce Base*
¼ cup milk
¼ cup grated Parmesan cheese
½ pound fettuccini noodles, cooked and drained
1 tablespoon chopped fresh parsley

In large skillet, melt butter; sauté mushrooms and onions until tender. Add ham; mix well. In small saucepan, make White Sauce Base*. Stir in ¼ cup additional milk and Parmesan cheese. Add ham mixture; heat until bubbly, stirring constantly. Serve over hot noodles. Garnish with parsley and additional grated Parmesan cheese, if desired. *Yield: 4 servings*

*White Sauce Base

2 tablespoons butter or margarine
2 tablespoons flour
¼ teaspoon salt
½ teaspoon **TABASCO® Pepper Sauce**
1 cup milk

Melt butter in saucepan over low heat. Blend in flour, salt and **TABASCO®**. Gradually stir in milk. Cook over medium heat, stirring constantly, until sauce thickens and comes to a boil. Simmer for 1 minute, continuing to stir. *Yield: About 1 cup*

Tomato and Basil Fettuccini

¼ cup chopped onion
1 clove garlic, minced
¼ cup olive oil
3½ cups (28-ounce can) peeled tomatoes (with liquid)
6 fresh basil leaves, chopped or 1 tablespoon dry basil
1 teaspoon salt
½ teaspoon pepper
1 box (12 ounces) **SAN GIORGIO® Fettuccini**, uncooked
Parmesan cheese (optional)

Sauté onion and garlic in oil in medium skillet until onion is tender, but not brown. Chop tomatoes into small pieces; reserve liquid. Add tomatoes, tomato liquid, basil, salt and pepper; bring to boil over medium heat. Reduce heat; simmer, uncovered, 15 to 20 minutes, stirring occasionally. Cook Fettuccini according to package directions; drain well. Immediately toss hot Fettuccini with tomato basil sauce in large serving dish. Garnish with Parmesan cheese, if desired. Serve.   *4 to 6 servings*

Summer—Spaghetti With Sausage and Zucchini

1 lb. **JIMMY DEAN® Sausage**
2 cans condensed cream of mushroom soup
1 cup milk
4 or 5 cups zucchini (about 1½ lbs.) quartered and sliced
¼ lb. mushrooms, sliced
¼ cup sliced green onions
½ tsp. salt
¼ tsp. pepper
1 lb. spaghetti
Parmesan cheese

Brown sausage in large skillet. Break up with fork. Add zucchini, mushrooms, green onions and sauté a few more minutes. Stir in soup, milk, salt and pepper. Cook over medium heat 15 minutes or until zucchini is tender. (Add more milk if the mixture becomes too thick). Cook spaghetti. Drain. Toss sausage mixture with cooked spaghetti & sprinkle generously with parmesan cheese.

Serves 6

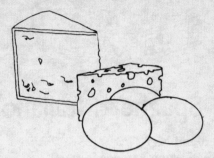

Spaghetti and Meat Balls With Enrico's Spaghetti Sauce

Prepare the meat balls as follows:

    1 lb. beef cubes ground
    ½ lb. shoulder pork ground
    1½ teaspoons salt
    ½ teaspoon black pepper
    ½ cup bread crumbs moistened with water
    ½ cup grated Italian style cheese
    1 teaspoon parsley
    1 medium onion, minced
    1 clove garlic, minced
    1 egg slightly beaten

Mix all above ingredients thoroughly. Shape into medium size balls and brown in about 3 tablespoons of fat. Add a little water to keep the meat balls from sticking and simmer for 15 minutes.

Add 1 jar of **ENRICO'S Spaghetti Sauce** and simmer just 5 minutes more. While the meat balls are simmering prepare the spaghetti by plunging it into rapidly boiling salted water for about 7 minutes or until tender. Drain and place on a flat dish or platter. Pour the **ENRICO'S Spaghetti Sauce** with meat balls over the spaghetti and sprinkle with grated Italian style cheese, if desired.

Four to six servings

Spaghetti Italiano

1 lb. ground beef
1 medium onion, chopped
½ green pepper, chopped
1 can (1-lb. or 2 cups) whole tomatoes, cut up
1 can (6-oz.) tomato paste
1 can (6-oz.) water
1 can (4-oz.) mushroom stems and pieces, undrained
2 teaspoons Worcestershire sauce
1 bay leaf
1 teaspoon salt
¼ teaspoon oregano
¼ teaspoon pepper
7-oz. package **CREAMETTE®** **Spaghetti**
2 tablespoons butter or margarine
Parmesan cheese

Brown meat, onion and green pepper till tender. Drain excess fat. Add all ingredients except spaghetti, butter and cheese. Simmer uncovered for 1 hour. Remove bay leaf. Prepare **CREAMETTE®** **Spaghetti** according to package directions. Drain. Toss with butter. Serve sauce over spaghetti with Parmesan cheese.

4 servings

VARIATION:

Spaghetti with meatballs: Prepare sauce as above, omitting ground beef. Combine beef, ½ cup chopped onion, 1 teaspoon salt, ¼ teaspoon pepper, ⅛ teaspoon garlic powder. Shape into 16 meatballs. Brown in 2 tablespoons oil. Drain. Add meatballs to sauce during last 25 minutes of cooking.

Linguine Quickie Pesto Sauce

1 lb. **RONZONI® Linguine #17** or **Spaghetti #8**
1 cup parsley finely chopped
½ cup basil finely chopped
½ cup pine nuts (optional)
2 cloves garlic finely chopped
½ cup olive oil
¼ cup water
½ cup Parmesan cheese
Dash pepper

Cook linguine as directed on package. While macaroni is cooking blend in mixing bowl parsley, basil, pine nuts, and garlic. When blended thoroughly together add olive oil, water, Parmesan cheese, and pepper. Mix. Combine mixture with cooked linguine; serve hot.

Spaghetti With White Clam Sauce

1 can (7½ ounces) minced clams
2 medium cloves garlic, minced
2 tablespoons chopped parsley
2 tablespoons butter or margarine
1 can (10¾ ounces) **CAMPBELL'S Condensed Cream of Mushroom Soup**
¼ cup milk or light cream
1 to 2 tablespoons grated Parmesan cheese
Cooked spaghetti

Drain clams; reserve liquid. In saucepan, cook clams, garlic, and parsley in butter a few minutes. Stir in soup, milk, clam liquid, and cheese. Cook over low heat 10 minutes. Stir occasionally. Serve over spaghetti. *Makes about 2 cups*

Posh Pasta

1 package (1½ oz.) **LAWRY'S® Spaghetti Sauce Mix With Imported Mushrooms**
1 can (6 oz.) tomato paste
1⅔ cups water
½ cup red wine
3 to 4 half chicken breasts, boned, skinned and cut into ½ × 2-inch strips (approximately 1½ cups)
6 ounces noodles or other pasta
1 can (8½ oz.) artichoke hearts, drained *OR* 1 package (10 oz.) frozen artichoke hearts, cooked according to package directions

In medium saucepan, combine **Spaghetti Sauce Mix With Imported Mushrooms**, tomato paste, water and wine; blend thoroughly. Cook, uncovered, for 10 minutes. Add chicken and simmer 15 minutes. Meanwhile, cook noodles according to package directions. Just before serving, add artichoke hearts to sauce and heat through. Serve over cooked noodles.

Makes 4 to 6 servings

Mushroom Lasagna

3 cans (3 oz.) **BinB® Sliced Mushrooms**, drained—reserving broth
1 package (16 oz.) lasagna noodles
1 package (8 oz.) cream cheese, softened
3 cups cottage cheese
1 tablespoon parsley flakes
½ teaspoon salt
½ teaspoon basil
¼ teaspoon oregano
⅛ teaspoon garlic powder
1 can (15 oz.) tomato sauce
¾ cup grated Parmesan cheese

Drain mushrooms, reserving buttery broth. Combine cream cheese, cottage cheese, salt, garlic powder and parsley. Set aside. Combine buttery broth, oregano, basil and tomato sauce and simmer about 10 minutes. Layer noodles and cheese mixture in buttered 9″ × 13″ shallow baking dish. Sprinkle each layer with 1 can of mushroom slices, tomato sauce and ¼ cup Parmesan cheese. Bake, covered, in preheated 350°F. oven for 30 minutes. Uncover and continue for 15 minutes.

Makes 8 to 10 servings

Worlds Fastest Lasagna

Brown in skillet:
> ½ lb. mild Italian sausage (May substitute hamburger)

Drain grease. Add:
> 1 15½ oz. jar spaghetti sauce

Mix:
> 1½ lb. ricotta cheese
> ¼ cup Parmesan cheese
> 1 egg
> 1 Tbsp. parsley flakes
> 1 tsp. salt

Slice:
> ½ lb. mozzarella cheese

Get out:
> **2 AZTECA® Super Size Flour Tortillas**

Using a 10″ skillet with ovenproof handle, place 1 tortilla in skillet. Top with one half ricotta, one half mozzarella, and one half the sauce. Repeat, forming a second layer. Bake in 375° oven 30 minutes. Let stand 10 minutes before serving (You may use square baking pan instead of skillet. Place tortilla in pan, tearing up second tortilla to fill in corners. Proceed as above).

Makes 6 servings

Lasagna With Mushrooms

1 (8-ounce) package **CREAMETTE® Italian Style
  Lasagna,** cooked as package directs and drained
1 pound lean ground beef *or* Italian sausage
1 cup chopped onion
3 cloves garlic, finely chopped
3½ cups tomato juice
8 ounces fresh mushrooms, sliced (about 2 cups)
1 (6-ounce) can tomato paste
1 tablespoon Worcestershire sauce
1 teaspoon oregano leaves
½ teaspoon salt
⅛ teaspoon pepper
1 (15- or 16-ounce) container ricotta cheese
1 cup grated Parmesan cheese
2 cups (8 ounces) shredded Mozzarella cheese
Parsley flakes

In large saucepan, brown meat; pour off fat. Add onion and garlic; cook and stir until onion is tender. Stir in tomato juice, mushrooms, tomato paste and seasonings. Cover; simmer 30 minutes, stirring occasionally. In 3-quart shallow baking dish (13 × 9-inch), layer half each of the cooked lasagna noodles, sauce, ricotta cheese, grated cheese and mozzarella cheese. Repeat layering; top with parsley. Cover tightly with foil; bake in preheated 350° oven 30 minutes or until bubbly. Uncover; bake 15 minutes longer. Remove from oven; let stand 20 minutes before serving. Refrigerate leftovers. *Makes 8 servings*

Tuna Lasagne

2 cans (6½ or 7 ounces) STAR-KIST® Tuna
½ cup chopped onion
2 cloves garlic, minced
1 can (15 ounces) tomato sauce
1 can (6 ounces) tomato paste
1 teaspoon sugar
1 teaspoon dried leaf oregano
½ teaspoon dried leaf basil
1 tablespoon lemon juice
½ package (8 ounces) lasagna noodles, cooked according
    to package directions
2 cups (1 pound) small curd creamed cottage cheese or
    ricotta cheese
1 pound mozzarella cheese, thinly sliced
1 cup (4 ounces) grated Parmesan cheese

Drain 1 tablespoon oil from **STAR-KIST® Tuna** into medium saucepan. Add onion and garlic. Cook until tender. Add tomato sauce, tomato paste, sugar, oregano, basil, and lemon juice. Simmer uncovered 45 minutes. Remove from heat, stir in **STAR-KIST® Tuna**. Spoon a small amount of sauce over bottom of a13 × 9 × 2-inch baking dish or shallow 3-quart casserole. Add layers of one-third noodles, one-third sauce, half the cottage cheese, and one-third mozzarella cheese . . . Repeat, ending with layers of noodles, sauce, and mozzarella cheese. Sprinkle Parmesan cheese over top. Bake in 350° oven 30 minutes. Let stand 10 minutes before serving. *Yield: 8 servings*

Lasagne Roll-Ups

4 quarts water
4 teaspoons salt
1 tablespoon oil
8 pieces **AMERICAN BEAUTY® Lasagne**
1 quart prepared spaghetti sauce
1 lb. Italian sausage or ground beef
¼ cup chopped onion
½ cup dry bread crumbs
1 teaspoon salt
½ teaspoon basil leaves
¼ teaspoon pepper
2 cups (8 oz.) shredded mozzarella cheese
12-oz. carton cottage cheese
1 egg, beaten
Grated Parmesan cheese, if desired

Heat oven to 350°F. Boil water in large deep pot with 4 teaspoons salt and oil (to prevent boiling over). Add lasagne; stir. Cook uncovered after water returns to a full rolling boil for 10 to 12 minutes. Stir occasionally. Drain and rinse under cold water.

Spread 2 cups of spaghetti sauce over bottom of 13 × 9-inch baking dish. In large skillet, brown sausage with onion over medium heat; drain. Add bread crumbs, 1 teaspoon salt, basil, pepper, mozzarella cheese, cottage cheese and egg. Cut each lasagne noodle in half crosswise; spread about 3 tablespoons of sausage mixture evenly on each half. Roll up from shorter side and place seam down in pan. Pour remaining sauce over top.

Cover and bake at 350°F. for 1 hour. Serve rolls with sauce. Serve with parmesan cheese, if desired.   *8 servings*

High Altitude—Above 3500 Feet: Cooking times may need to be increased slightly for lasagne; no additional changes.

NUTRITIONAL INFORMATION PER SERVING

SERVING SIZE: ⅛ of recipe		PERCENT U.S. RDA	
Calories	536	PER SERVING	
Protein	25 g	Protein	39
Carbohydrate	37 g	Vitamin A	6
Fat	32 g	Vitamin C	—
Sodium	1429 mg	Thiamine	22
Potassium	113 mg	Riboflavin	30
		Niacin	13
		Calcium	32
		Iron	20

Homestyle Canneloni Classico

1½ pounds ground beef
1 small onion, chopped
1 package (10 oz.) frozen chopped spinach, cooked and
  squeezed dry
1½ cups (6 oz.) shredded mozzarella cheese, divided
½ cup bread crumbs
1 egg, slightly beaten
¼ cup grated Parmesan cheese, divided
1 teaspoon oregano
½ teaspoon salt
¼ teaspoon black pepper
1 jar (15½ oz.) **RAGU´® Homestyle Spaghetti Sauce**,
  any flavor
½ pound (about 8) lasagna noodles, cooked and drained

Preheat oven to 350°F. In large skillet, brown beef; add onion and
sauté until translucent. Pour off fat. Add spinach, 1 cup mozzarella, bread crumbs, egg, ½ cheese and seasonings. Mix well;
set aside. In 11″ × 7″ baking dish, spread 1 cup **Homestyle**
Spaghetti Sauce. Cut each lasagna noodle in half crosswise.
Place quarter cup of filling on each noodle half; roll and place
seam-side down in baking dish. Pour remaining sauce over canne-
loni; sprinkle with remaining cheeses. Cover tightly with foil; bake
30 minutes. Uncover, bake 5 minutes more.   *Serves 8*

The King's Noodle

3 cups cooked, drained egg noodles
2 cans **KING OSCAR Sardines**, drained, reserving oil
¼ cup melted butter
2 Tbsp. lemon juice
Salt
Parsley
Lemon wedges

Combine reserved sardine oil, salt, butter, lemon juice. Stir into
cooked noodles. Place mixture in serving dish. Garnish with
sardines around edges, and if you wish, parsley. Serve with lemon
wedges.

Mueller's® Chicken Tetrazzini

1 can (4 ounces) sliced mushrooms, drained, reserving
  liquid
⅓ cup chopped onion
4 tablespoons butter or margarine
3 tablespoons flour
1½ cups chicken broth
½ cup light cream
½ teaspoon salt
Dash pepper
½ cup dry vermouth or chicken broth
¾ cup grated Parmesan cheese
8 ounces **MUELLER'S® Thin Spaghetti**
2 cups diced cooked chicken

In saucepan, cook mushrooms and onion in butter until soft; stir in flour. Gradually add 1½ cups broth, cream and reserved mushroom liquid; cook, stirring, until sauce thickens. Remove from heat. Add salt, pepper, vermouth and ¼ cup of the cheese; set aside. Meanwhile, cook spaghetti as directed on package; drain. Combine spaghetti and chicken in 2-quart casserole; pour sauce over and mix lightly. Sprinkle with remaining cheese. Bake at 375°F. for 20 minutes or until bubbling.   *4 to 6 servings*

Ideal Choo Choo-Wheels With Meat Sauce

1 Tbsp. salad oil
1 small onion, chopped
1 clove garlic, finely chopped
1-lb. ground beef
½ tsp. salt
⅛ tsp. pepper
1 tsp. oregano
Dash of cinnamon
1-8 oz. can tomato sauce
1 (No. 303) can tomatoes
1 pkg. **IDEAL Choo Choo-Wheels**
Parmesan cheese

② Tangy Barbecue Beans

One 16-oz. can Van Camp's,
    Pork and Beans
One 7-oz. can luncheon meat,
    cubed

¼ cup apricot preserves
2 tablespoons barbecue sauce

Combine all ingredients; simmer 10 to 15 minutes or until thickened. FIVE ½
CUP SERVINGS

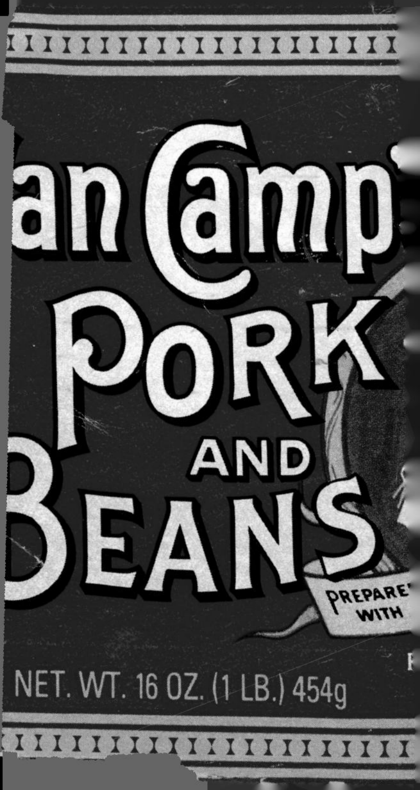
an Camp'
PORK
AND
BEANS
PREPARE
WITH
NET. WT. 16 OZ. (1 LB.) 454g

Heat salad oil over medium heat. Add onion, garlic and beef. Cook, stirring beef until browned. Add tomatoes and cook for 5 minutes. Add tomato sauce, salt, pepper, oregano, cinnamon and simmer for 30 minutes stirring occasionally. Meanwhile, cook **IDEAL Choo Choo-Wheels** according to package directions. Drain. Serve **IDEAL Choo Choo-Wheels** topped with meat sauce, sprinkled with Parmesan cheese. *Serves 4-6*

Deep Dish Pizza-A-Roni

1 pkg. (8 oz.) **GOLDEN GRAIN® Beef Flavor RICE-A-RONI®**
2 Tbsp. butter or margarine
2¾ cups hot water
1 cup grated Cheddar cheese
1 cup spaghetti sauce
8 slices Jack cheese
2 Italian sausage, cooked and sliced
2 Tbsp. grated Parmesan cheese
1 can (2½ oz.) sliced mushrooms, drained

Prepare **RICE-A-RONI®** with butter and water, according to package directions. Let stand until all liquid is absorbed. Fold in Cheddar cheese. Spread into 10-inch pie plate. Bake at 450°F. for 5 minutes to set crust. Top with spaghetti sauce, sliced cheese, sausage, Parmesan, mushrooms. Top with additional sauce, if desired. Bake at 450°F. for 10 minutes or until lightly brown. Let stand 5 minutes before cutting into 8 wedges.

Eggs

Poached Eggs With Tarragon & Yogurt

6 poached eggs
2 cups DANNON® **Plain Yogurt**
1 tsp. paprika
2 tsp. chopped tarragon-½ tsp. dried
Salt and pepper to taste

Arrange eggs on hot serving dish. In saucepan, mix yogurt, paprika and tarragon. Salt and pepper to taste. Stir over low heat until warm. Spoon over eggs. Garnish with parsley.

Makes 3 servings

Golden Eggs in a Nest

6 hard-cooked eggs, cut in half
½ cup finely chopped cooked ham
¼ cup mayonnaise
4 teaspoons FRENCH'S® **Prepared Mustard**
1 package (10-oz.) frozen chopped spinach, thawed and well drained
3 cups cooked rice
1 tablespoon lemon juice
2 tablespoons butter or margarine, melted
1 envelope FRENCH'S® **Cheese Sauce Mix**
1 cup milk

Remove yolks from eggs; mash. Combine with ham, mayonnaise, and 3 teaspoons of the mustard. Stuff egg whites. Combine spinach, rice, lemon juice, and butter; spoon into a shallow 1½-quart casserole or six individual casseroles. Top with stuffed eggs. Prepare sauce mix using milk and stirring in 1 teaspoon mustard; spoon over casserole. Bake at 350°F. for 20 minutes, until hot.

6 servings

Huevos California

1 tablespoon butter or margarine
½ cup frozen **ORE-IDA® Potatoes O'Brien**
¼ teaspoon salt
¼ teaspoon chili powder
2 eggs beaten
2 tablespoons sour cream
1 tablespoon taco sauce (optional)
1 teaspoon chopped green onions
1 large (9 inch) flour tortilla

1. In skillet over medium heat (350°F.) melt butter, add potatoes, salt and chili powder; cook until potatoes are tender. Stir occasionally. Add eggs, scramble with potatoes until set.
2. Briefly warm tortilla in dry frying pan over very low heat, turning often. Place egg mixture on tortilla; top with sour cream, taco sauce and sprinkle of green onions. Fold the two sides envelope fashion, and roll up, garnish with additional sour cream and green onions. *Yield: 1 serving*

Egg Croquettes

1 can (10¾ ounces) **CAMPBELL'S Condensed Cream of Celery Soup**
8 hard-cooked eggs, finely chopped
¼ cup fine dry bread crumbs
2 tablespoons finely chopped onion
2 tablespoons finely chopped parsley
Dash pepper
2 tablespoons shortening
⅓ to ½ cup milk

Mix *thoroughly* 2 tablespoons soup, eggs, bread crumbs, onion, parsley and pepper. Shape *firmly* into 8 croquettes or patties. (If mixture is difficult to handle, chill before shaping.) Roll in additional bread crumbs. In skillet, brown croquettes in shortening. Meanwhile, in saucepan, combine remaining soup and milk. Heat; stir occasionally. Serve with croquettes.

Makes 6 to 8 servings

Eggs San Remo

1 clove garlic (or equivalent garlic powder)
½ cup chicken stock (or ½ cup water and chicken
flavored bouillon)
1½ tablespoons butter or margarine
1 tablespoon flour (plus additional flour for tomatoes)
½ cup **MILNOT®**
4 thick slices underripe tomato
2 eggs, poached
4 or more tablespoons grated Parmesan or shredded
Cheddar cheese
Fat for frying

Simmer clove of garlic in chicken stock about 3 minutes; remove
garlic. Make a sauce: melt butter, stir in tablespoon of flour, blend
in chicken stock, stir in **MILNOT®**. Continue cooking and stirring until sauce is thickened.

Dip tomatoes in flour. Sauté quickly in small amount of fat until
browned on both sides; place in shallow baking dish. Place one
poached egg on two tomato slices. Pour sauce over eggs, sprinkle
with cheese. Place under broiler until cheese melts.

Yield: 2 servings

Vegetable-Cheese Omelet

1 package (10 oz.) **BIRDS EYE® AMERICANA
RECIPE® Vegetables, Wisconsin Country Style**
½ cup diced cheddar cheese
6 eggs
¼ teaspoon salt
2 tablespoons milk or water
2 tablespoons butter or margarine

Prepare vegetables as directed on package. Stir in cheese and the
topping and keep warm. Beat eggs with salt and milk. Heat butter
in skillet. Add egg mixture and cook over medium heat. Run a
spatula slowly around the edge to allow uncooked portion to flow
underneath. When omelet is set but still glossy, top with vegetable
mixture and cook 1 to 2 minutes longer. Loosen with spatula, fold
over and turn onto platter. *Makes 3 servings*

Note: ¼ cup of the cooked vegetables may be reserved and spooned over filled omelet as garnish, if desired.

Gourmet French Omelet

2 2½-oz. jars sliced mushrooms, drained
3 tablespoons **PARKAY Margarine**
6 eggs, beaten
⅓ cup milk
Salt and pepper
¾ cup (3 ozs.) shredded **CRACKER BARREL Brand Sharp Natural Cheddar Cheese**
1 teaspoon finely chopped chives

Sauté mushrooms in 1 tablespoon margarine. Melt remaining margarine in 10-inch skillet over low heat. Combine eggs, milk and seasonings; pour into skillet. Cook slowly. As egg mixture sets, lift slightly with a spatula to allow uncooked portion to flow underneath. Cover omelet with ½ cup cheese, mushrooms and chives; fold in half and sprinkle with remaining cheese.

3 to 4 servings

Sausage Quiche

½ lb. **BOB EVANS FARMS® Roll Sausage**
1 unbaked 9-in. pie crust
1 tsp. butter
1 medium onion, chopped
½ cup grated Swiss cheese
4 eggs
1 cup milk
1 cup heavy cream
½ tsp. salt
¼ tsp. pepper

Crumble sausage and cook until brown. Remove sausage and add butter and onions to drippings. Cook for five minutes. Cover bottom of pie crust with sausage, onions and ¼ cup cheese. In mixing bowl combine remaining cheese, eggs, milk, cream, salt and pepper. Mix well and pour over sausage mixture. Bake at 425° for 15 minutes. Reduce heat to 350° and continue baking until brown and well set (approximately 20 minutes longer).

Serves 6

Special Thanks

We would like to thank the following companies and organizations listed for the use of their recipes.

American Home Foods
Armour and Co.
Atalanta/Krakus/Polka—Atalanta Corp.
Azteca Corn Products Corp.
Baltimore Spice Co., The
Banquet Foods Corp.
Batterlite Whitlock Inc.
Bays English Muffin Corp.
Bertolli U.S.A.
Best Foods
Blue Ribbon®—Continental Nut Co.
Bob Evans Farms
Booth Fisheries Corp.
Borden Inc.
Bordo Products Co.
Brownberry
Campbell Soup Co.
Canada Dry Corp.
Castle & Cooke Foods
Cheez-Ola®—Fisher Cheese Co.
Chesebrough-Pond's Inc.
Clorox Co., The
Colonial Sugars, Inc.
Cookin' Good™—Showell Farms, Inc.
Country Pride Foods Ltd.
Country Smoked Meats Inc.
Creamette Co., The
Cumberland Packing Corp.
Dannon Co., Inc., The
Del Monte Corp.
Diet Shasta®—Shasta Beverages
Domino®—Amstar Corp.
Durkee Foods—Div. of SCM Corp.
Eckrich, Peter, & Sons, Inc.
Enrico's—Ventre Packing Co., Inc.
Estee Corp., The
E-Z-Bake Flour—Acme Evans Co.
Farmland Foods, Inc.
Farm-Raised Catfish—Catfish Farmers of America
Featherweight®—Chicago Dietetic Supply, Inc.
Fisher Nut Co.
French, R.T., Co., The
Frito-Lay, Inc.
Gebhardt Mexican Foods
General Foods Corp.
General Mills, Inc.
Golden Dipt. Co.
Golden Grain Macaroni Co.
Grandma's®—Duffy-Mott Co., Inc.

Health Valley Natural Foods
Heinz U.S.A.
Herb-Ox®—The Pure Food Co.
High Liner®—National Sea Products
Hillshire Farm®—Kahn's and Co.
Holland House Brands Co.
Holly Farms Poultry Industries, Inc.
Hormel, Geo. A., & Co.
Hunt-Wesson Kitchens
Ideal Macaroni Co.
Imperial Sugar Co.
International Multifoods
Jays Foods, Inc.
Jennie-O Foods, Inc.
Jimmy Dean Meat Co., Inc.
John Morrell & Co.
Jones Dairy Farm
Keebler Co.
Kellogg Company
Kikkoman International, Inc.
King Oscar Fine Foods
Kraft, Inc.
La Choy Food Products
La Fiesta™—Fiesta Foods, Inc.
Land O' Lakes, Inc.
Lawry's Foods, Inc.
Lea & Perrins
Libby, McNeill & Libby, Inc.
Lindsay International Inc.
Lipton, Thomas J., Inc.
Lucky Leaf®—Knouse Foods Cooperative, Inc.
Meadow Gold Dairies
Milnot Co.
Morton Salt
Mr. & Mrs."T" Products
Mrs. Paul's Kitchens, Inc.
Mueller Co., C. F.
Nabisco Brands, Inc.
National Duckling Council
Ore-Ida Foods, Inc.
Ortega—Heublein/Grocery Products Group
Oscar Mayer Foods Corp.
Pepperidge Farm, Inc.
Perdue Farms Inc.
Peter Pan Seafoods
Pet Inc.
Pillsbury Co., The
Pompeian, Inc.

Procter & Gamble—Foods Div.
Progresso Quality Foods
Ralston Purina Co.
Rath Packing Co., The
Rhodes™—Dakota Bake-N-Serv, Inc.
Roman Meal Co.
Ronzoni Macaroni Co., Inc.
Rosarita Mexican Foods Co.
Rus-ettes—Idaho Frozen Foods
S&W Fine Foods, Inc.
San Giorgio-Skinner
Smucker, J. M. Co., The
Star-Kist Foods, Inc.
Stokely-Van Camp, Inc.
Success®—Riviana Foods, Inc.
Sun-Diamond Growers of Calif.

Sunkist Growers, Inc.
Sunshine Biscuits, Inc.
Swift & Co.
Tabasco®—McIlhenny Co.
Taylor, John W., Packing Co., Inc.
Tennessee Pride® Odom Sausage
   Co., Inc.
Tyson Foods, Inc.
Uncle Ben's Foods
Underwood, Wm., Co.
Veg-All®—The Larsen Co.
Wakefield® Pacific Pearl Seafoods
Welch Foods Inc.
Wile, Julius, Sons & Co., Inc.
Wilson Foods Corp.
Wolf Brand Products

Index